New Brunswick Theological Seminary
New Brunswick, New Jersey

Using Transformational Preaching to Bring Awareness and
Break the Silence in Congregations regarding Sexual and
Physical Abuse against Women

by
Marcia Rachelle Grayson

Has been approved by the Committee of Readers and has
been accepted by the Director of the Gardner A. Sage
Library and the Committee on behalf of the Faculty of
New Brunswick Theological Seminary
in partial fulfillment of the requirements of the degree of

Doctor of Ministry
in
Transformational Preaching

FOR THE COMMITTEE READERS

The Reverend Faye Banks Taylor, D. Min., Academic Advisor

The Reverend Raynard Smith, Ph.D. ,
Reader and Associate Professor

T. Patrick Milas, Ph.D. , Director of Gardner A. Sage Library
May 2019

**Using Transformational Preaching to Bring Awareness
and Break the Silence in Congregations
regarding Sexual and Physical Abuse against Women**

A Dissertation
Submitted in Partial Fulfillment
of the Requirements for the Degree
of Doctor of Ministry
in Transformational Preaching
at New Brunswick Theological Seminary
New Brunswick, New Jersey
Spring 2019

MARCIA RACHELLE GRAYSON

DISSERTATION COMMITTEE
Dr. Faye Banks Taylor, Advisor

Dr. Carol Lynn Patterson, Director of Doctor of
Ministry Program

Xulon Press
2301 Lucien Way #415
Maitland, FL 32751
407.339.4217
www.xulonpress.com

Unless otherwise indicated, Scripture quotations taken from the New Revised Standard Version (NRSV). Copyright © 1989 the Division of Christian Education of the National Council of the Churches of Christ in the United States of America.

Paperback ISBN-13: 978-1-6628-2965-9
eBook ISBN-13: 978-1-6628-2966-6

Table of Contents

Abstract vii

Acknowledgments ix

Foreword By Dr. Semaj Vanzant, Sr. xiii

Introduction xv

Chapter One
Statement of the Problem and Analysis for Study. 1

Limitations and Delimitations. 12

Chapter Two
Literature Review. 17

Chapter Three
Methodology 37

Chapter Four
Implementation of the Project. 47

The Scriptures and Sermons. 55

Chapter Five
Reflections, Summary of Results, and Conclusion 95

Appendix A
Curriculum Vitae. 117

Appendix B
Covenant Team Members. 119

Appendix C
Informed Consultants. 123

Appendix D

    Survey Questionnaires 125

Appendix E

    Consent Forms. 153

Appendix F

    Scriptures and Sermons, Orders of Service 161

Appendix G

    Public Information 207

    Bibliography 209

Abstract

This research project primarily explores the use of transformational preaching to impact consciousness by bringing awareness and piercing the silence of congregations concerning sexual and physical abuse against women. These transformative sermons address those problematic, challenging, and controversial Scriptures pertaining to violent abuses against women from a non-patriarchal perspective. In addition, this research project addresses two questions: Does the use of transformative sermons promote a change in the congregation's awareness of the importance of breaking the silence within the church, and does the use of transformational sermons promote a community that affirms women in the congregation who have been detrimentally affected by such atrocities?[1] Further, this project aims to dismantle the silence and lack of appropriate responses from convention leaders, preachers, church leaders, and congregations.

---

[1] The term affirm means to acknowledge publicly that what happened to the women is wrong, is not their fault, and the church is listening to them.

Acknowledgments

G iving all glory and honor to my Lord and Savior Jesus, the Christ, and for the infinite wisdom of God, who called and anointed me for such a time as this, for opening up the door for my admission into this awesome transformational preaching cohort, and for loving me, I give thanks. Thank you, Holy Spirit, for always guiding me and empowering me. I give thanks to God for my father in the ministry, Rev. Dr. William A. Greene, Jr., for praying and encouraging me to press on in the application and admission stages of this academic journey. Thank you to Rev. Dr. Lorna Wilson for also being an integral part of the journey, for being a friend, an encourager, and co-laborer. We did it, Lorna, you, me, and "monkey!"

Special thanks and love for my parents, James and Katrina Walker, my family for your love, encouragement, support, and assistance in every way imaginable, and my grandmother, "Nanny," you would be so proud. To Desiree and Aunt Marie Pendleton, thank you for opening your home and providing food for my formation meetings, and to Bettye F. Hayes and Yvonne Adams for pushing me to greater depths and higher heights as my best "sistah-friends." Much appreciation to my covenant team members, Glenn Johnson, Desiree Pendleton, Jaikia Fair, Ernestine Counts, Jennell Jackson, Minister Kerwin Webb, and Gary Bailey, for thinking it not robbery to assist and encourage me, for sharing your gifts and talents, love for and dedication to my success. Glenn, I offer a special thanks for being my sounding board during frustrating moments and for always being there to help with absolutely everything.

Much love and appreciation to the leaders and members of Second Baptist Church of Asbury Park. I am eternally grateful to each of you and those from the surrounding churches who supported the "Hour of Power" weekly worship experiences and surveys. Also, to the focus group members, I appreciate your openness, transparency, support, and willingness to be open for healing and transformation. Thank you all for becoming a loving and affirming community. Thanks to all who prayed; to Holli Cox for printing out *everything* and for creating the emergency help agencies and announcement cards for disbursement; to all the agencies and counselors who attended and assisted each week: Displaced Homemakers' Service, Mercy Center, 180° Turning Lives Around, Jackson Counseling Services, Ernestine Counts, and Lonjete Nias. Lastly, I thank my pastor, Rev. Dr. Semaj Y. Vanzant, Sr., for your love, encouragement, support, and commitment to intentionally promote my project and me in every arena. Thank you for your leadership, your confidence, and for opening the doors of the church for this project while exposing and encouraging the congregation to participate and become change agents through this work in our community.

Thank you to the New Brunswick Theological Seminary faculty and staff for your support and contribution to my successful completion of the course work and research project. Dr. Faye Taylor, my advisor, I truly could not have completed this journey without you. Your faithful dedication, prayers, assurances, and fervor to my success and sanity are deeply appreciated. Thank you for always telling me to breathe. To Mrs. Kathleen Hart Brumm, thank you for being my editor and for your diligent work and encouragement. Also, to Dr. Lorena Parrish, Ph.D. , I thank you for pushing me in the direction of my passion and not settling for less.

Lastly, to "The Remnant," the inaugural transformational preaching cohort at NBTS. I appreciate you all embracing me, showing me family love and encouragement, and for our forever bond. Jerome and Antonio, thank you for always opening your pulpits to me to complete my preaching assignments, to practice on and learn from your beautiful congregations. As we always said in class (Lorna), "Iron sharpens iron." You all have helped to shape and sharpen me, but most importantly, you all helped me to discover my voice and myself. In doing so, I've become "the voice of broken women." I love you all. Thank you.

Foreword
By Dr. Semaj Vanzant, Sr.

In the early 2000's Verizon ran a commercial to advertise the quality of their cell phone service. The main character in the commercial was shown in different places, countries, parts of a building showing that no matter where he was, he was able to get reception. He did this by asking one question: Can you hear me now? Almost with every step he took, he would ask this same question to the person he was talking too: Can you hear me now? In every place where he went, he asked this same question, can you hear me now?

The question—can you hear me now? —was not asked to annoy or frustrate the person on the other end, it was simply a question of clarification to verify that the cell phone reception promised was the cell phone reception received.

In this groundbreaking work, Rev. Dr. Marcia R. Grayson highlights the fact that the reception for voices of women who have been physically, emotionally, mentally, psychologically abused has not been what was promised. In this book Dr. Grayson helps us to hear the voices of these women, not just in the audio, but with a heart of compassion, a mind of understanding, and a spirit of intercession so that women who are violated will know or at least come to know that their voices are being heard.

As Dr. Grayson's pastor I have seen her wrestle with the season in which her own voice was not heard. I have also witnessed the healing she has received from making the hard choice to embrace this process of going through the pain to get to the place where healing happens.

Henri J. M. Nouwen would call Dr. Grayson a "wounded healer" because her ministry has brought freedom and liberation to those who have been afflicted and negatively affected by these heinous acts of violation against them. Her preaching is nothing short of transformational in its ability to make practical the spiritual and make space for God to *"heal the broken hearted and bind up their wounds"* (Psalm 147:3).

Not only does Dr. Grayson speak with a priestly voice to the women whose voices have not been heard, she also speaks prophetically to the system of patriarchy, male dominance, and chauvinism that has plagued this and every society since almost the beginning of human history. This system that in many ways has denied the humanity of women, thus devaluing her right to speak and her right to be heard. Dr. Grayson's boldness coupled with her prophetic imagination in sermonic genius sounds a clarion call for equality and justice so that the voices of women who have previously been made to suffer in silence are now able to find deliverance in meaningful dialogue.

I sincerely believe that once you grasp what the Spirit of the Lord has given to Dr. Grayson through her personal, professional, and preaching journey evident in this finished work, women whose voices have been silenced will be empowered to speak out and those who have not suffered this violation of person will be emboldened to create the space so that we can eliminate the need for anyone to ask again: Can't You Hear Her?

Dr. Semaj Vanzant, Sr.
Pastor-Teacher
Second Baptist Church
Asbury Park, NJ

Introduction

There are many women who have been physically or sexually violated who attend virtually every church across the world. Some have endured and are still enduring violent physical abuse: spousal abuse, partner abuse, incestuous abuse, mental abuse, emotional abuse and/or neglect, and various types of sexual abuses and violations. Unfortunately, not every woman has or has had an affirming space in which to speak of these atrocities that have silenced or dismissed their experiences, voices, tears, and peace. Too often, those who have been victimized are told never to speak of the violations committed against them. Their voices are silenced. Like Tamar and Dinah, they are forced to process their trauma and grief alone and weep in solitude, forever holding on to their shameful secrets. [2,3] Any actions taken on their behalf were incapable of restoring their good names and dignity. These secrets become like a cancer, eating away at their emotional, psychological, and spiritual cores a little at a time. Once that bedrock is disabled or obliterated, their subconscious minds suppress the traumatic memories long enough for them to try to survive one more day.

For many years, the church has been largely silent on these issues. This is not to say that the church has not responded to the cry of those who have had the courage to finally break the silence and say, "Enough is enough!" However, hardly has there

---

[2] The Holy Bible, New Revised Standard Version. 2 Samuel 13. All scriptural references will be from the NRSV unless otherwise noted. Superscript numbers embedded in the text are verse numbers.

[3] Genesis 34.

been a word preached from the pulpit regarding these violent assaults committed against women: women in the congregation, women in the community, or women in the society at large (with the exception of Bishop T.D. Jakes⁴). This project uses transformational preaching to dismantle, from the pulpit, the church's silence, freeing the congregation to assist, affirm, and positively impact the lives of women within the worship community who have been physically and sexually violated. This allows the church to offer godly love that affirms abused women's experience and finally no longer ignores the violence against them.

Additionally, these sermons encourage preachers to respond from the pulpit, to use transformative preaching to address the sensitive and "taboo" issues of sex, abuse, and heinous acts against women. As a result, the congregation receives biblical and scriptural references that equip them to be an informed and supportive community.

Isaiah 61:1–3 is the thematic scripture for this research project:

> The Spirit of the Lord God is upon me, because the Lord has anointed me to bring good news to the poor; he has sent me to bind up the brokenhearted, to proclaim liberty to the captives, and the opening of the prison to those who are bound; to proclaim the year of the Lord's favor, and the day of vengeance of our God; to comfort all who mourn; to grant to those who mourn in Zion — to give them a beautiful headdress instead of ashes, the oil of gladness instead of mourning, the garment of praise instead of a faint spirit; that they may be called oaks of righteousness, the planting of the Lord, that he may be glorified.

---

⁴ Woman Thou Art Loosed is a ministry created by Bishop T.D. Jakes, addressing, from the pulpit and in conferences, the hurts of women who have been sexually, physically, emotionally, mentally, or spiritually violated.

Chapter One establishes the foundation for this project through a description and analysis of the problem, which is the church's lack of awareness and alarming silence pertaining to sexual and physical violence against women. It includes the thesis and, for clarity, a brief definition of terms used throughout the document by this researcher. The chapter also shares some personal experiences of abuse, which help inform the reader why this topic is of such significance.

Chapter Two provides a description of the biblical, theological, and pastoral issues to be addressed. In addition, it documents the resources that informed the sermons, worship experiences, and group discussions. These references ensure clarity and optimum efficiency in addressing the issues.

Chapter Three discloses the methodology used for the "Hour of Power" worship services, the focus group discussions, the surveys that were implemented, and the variations of homiletical and hermeneutical methods used for the four transformational sermons preached in the series.

Chapter Four furnishes the implementation, analysis, and evaluation of the impact of this research project. It assesses, as well, the effectiveness of transformational preaching to bring awareness and break the silence in congregations regarding sexual and physical violence against women.

Chapter Five offers reflections on personal and congregational transformations, summarizes the issue, and presents the information gained through using surveys. It also evaluates portions of the project that might have provided better clarity of intent. Lastly, the researcher shares the achievements, expectations, and surprises of the project, and proposes future ministry endeavors because of this study.

CHAPTER ONE

Statement of the Problem and Analysis for Study

H aving been reared by a woman engulfed by hurt and having been hurt myself, I am very passionate and concerned about the epidemic of secrecy around the internal injuries done to women in our families, churches, and communities. I protest the lack of transformative sermons that address the issues of violated women. There are women in our various contexts that are hurting, holding in painful stories of mental, physical, and emotional abuse, including rape, incest, abandonment, and other victimizations. These continue to hold them captive spiritually, emotionally, mentally, and in some cases, physically. Abused women hiding in our congregations need affirmation, encouragement, and emotional support from pastors, church leaders, and fellow congregants to assist them in processing the explosive effects of abuse so they may experience the love of God through the church. Transformational preaching, which impacts and promotes effective behavioral change, will bring awareness to the church, help congregants understand the presence of these offenses, break the silence surrounding violence against women, and bring its detrimental effects to the fore in their communities.

Description of Context

My own story serves as a catalyst for this research project. I was reared in a home with a father who was physically abusive to my mother. Eventually, my mother and I escaped from Hawaii, where we lived with my father, and came back to New Jersey, where my maternal grandmother resided. She was responsible for getting us safely back to the mainland. My mother was not alone in being physically abused. My close cousin was also abused by her husband. Her husband was *extremely* abusive to her physically, mentally, and emotionally. He, too, had multiple adulterous affairs. Unfortunately, I was a witness to my male cousin's abusive behavior throughout my life from childhood to young adulthood. Finally, his abuse ceased when he got "saved"—that is, when he began to change his ways because of his conviction to follow Christ's teachings, which happened about a year or two before illness took his life.

Abuse pervaded my extended family. My uncle, my mother's brother, was also abusive to his now recovering alcoholic wife. I describe her like this because alcoholism was her reasoning for why he would hit her at times. As she would describe his abuse, she would say things like, "I provoked him," and "He would pop me one, and I would go sit down." To me, there was no excuse for his behavior. Lastly, I had a cousin who had a violent live-in boyfriend who physically abused her. She ran to escape from him while her eight-year-old son attempted to restrain him, but he struck her son down. As she was running down the porch step, the abuser pushed her, and she fell, hit her head, went into a coma, and died shortly after. This was a lot for me and, I would argue, for anyone to process. Most times, children of the abused are overlooked, and they are rarely, if ever, given the opportunity to have their voices heard, stories told, emotions processed, and spirits healed. They are either threatened or intimidated by their abusers, and often, family members and others insist that everything must remain a secret. They may also be too ashamed to tell and assume the blame themselves.[5] As a result, some children grow up to become abusers themselves, the classic "abused-abuser."[6] They are adults who are hurting and/or those who overcompensate for being helpless as a child.

Adding to the hurt and pain I endured as a child, I was molested at a young age by a teenage boy, the son of my babysitter. She used to leave him to watch her youngest two sons and me while she ran errands. When I would need to go to the bathroom, I was ordered to come out of the room with my pants and panties down, so that he and his little brothers could look at me. I was then threatened with a belt and coerced to lie on the bed face down, and the belt would be slapped on the bed next to me, creating an unfathomable amount of fear deep within my psyche. I attempted to tell my mother once, and he (the teenage boy) punished me when he and a neighbor let my pet rabbit out of her cage and had the neighbor's dog track her down and kill her. My father found my rabbit mangled with her leash still attached to what was left of her neck. Stunned into silence, I held this secret of my molestation and torment for many years until my mother remarried and became pregnant with my youngest brother.

My mother had remarried after the death of my father. My fear was that the baby, if it was a girl, would go to the babysitter who was taking care of my younger brother. It was the same type of environment in which I was molested: a teenage boy and two younger boys. To save her from my fate, I promised to quit school

---

[5] https://www.secasa.com.au/pages/feelings-after-sexual-assault/.

[6] Kutuk, Meryem Ozlem, et al. "Abused-Abuser Dilemma in Sexual Abuse and Forensic Evaluation: a Case Report." Dusunen Adam: Journal of Psychiatry & Neurological Sciences 30, no. 2 (June 2017): 145–148. Academic Search Premier, EBSCOhost (accessed June 7, 2018).

to care for her. Because of how serious the situation was to me, with tears flowing, I finally revealed to my mother the horrifying details of how I had been abused. She held me, we cried, and we never spoke of it again. My birth father died, never knowing what had happened to me.

Years later, at MegaFest, Dr. Claudette Copeland was preaching one of the breakout sessions for women.[7] She began speaking of women as victims of abuse and violent sexual crimes. I remembered thinking that I had picked the wrong breakout session because I could not identify with these women, not even my close friend who was seated next to me. Suddenly, the Spirit brought back to my remembrance my abuser. Years before, I had plotted to find him and do him harm. I worked in a county jail and had access to criminal databases. I knew if he did this to me as a teenager, for sure, he must have grown into a sexual predator, must have gotten caught, and must be in the system for me to find him. The Holy Spirit confronted me with all of this, bringing it from the deepest recesses of my mind. As I moved to the center aisle toward the altar, I began shouting at the top of my lungs as loud as I could, eyes closed, head back, looking up toward heaven, screaming, "I HATE HIM, I HATE HIM, I HATE HIM!" repeatedly until I could feel the hand of God reaching into the bowels of my soul and pulling out the root of all my anger. It had the sound and feeling of uprooting a clump of weeds. I was being purged, spitting up a clear substance, until I no longer felt the anger and the rage. Immediately after, I felt peace and a calmness. I knew that I had been delivered. From that moment on, I have never been able to remember my abuser's last name, and neither can my mother. At that moment, I came to know God as Jehovah-Rapha (the God who heals) for myself.

---

[7] MegaFest is a spiritually powerful family-friendly ministry conference bringing together men, women, and children given by T.D. Jakes Ministries.

It is this experience, namely, the healing from a secret and hurtful violation of my childhood innocence and physical being through a transformational sermon, which births this research project. There are many women who are aching, who have had to suppress their experiences of violence and embarrassing, damaging, evil offenses against them. They have never had the opportunity to come to terms with what happened, to find a place to heal, or to come to know the God who heals and restores through the transformative power of the preached Word.

The time of my deliverance was the beginning of my healing process. I began to understand why I am the way that I am, and especially the way I was back then. I suffered from very low self-esteem, was ashamed of my body, and was overly protective of others (especially women) who I believed needed protection. In addition, I was very defensive in my demeanor, aggressive against men who I felt were intimidating, promiscuous, and involved in broken relationships. I felt like the Samaritan woman at the well, except I was naïve about sexual matters.[8] I was fearful of abandonment and emotionally dysfunctional. As God pulled the root of hatred and anger out of me, it was as if the layers of an onion had begun to open in me like a blooming onion appetizer.[9] As God began to reveal the effects of the suppressed hurt, each of its results began to peel off as God started healing the broken spaces and places in my life.

There are many women who are bitter, angry, miserable, unapproachable, depressed, unforgiving, and broken in their spirit who do not know or understand the root of their feelings, or how such feelings are related to the hurtful violations that they have

---

[8] John 4:7–26.

[9] An onion is cored and sliced 7/8 of the way down its sides, then battered. As the onion is fried, the layers open up, making it easier to pull off small pieces of the onion for eating.

compartmentalized in the recesses of their subconscious. They are also unaware of how to release the effects of the offenses. It was the transformational sermon of Dr. Claudette Copeland that enabled me to begin the healing process, embrace forgiveness, and be transformed from the inside out. Unfortunately, I have not found any further experiences within the church or from any other preacher that acknowledge or address violence against women openly from the pulpit. This leads me to think that many women are not being exposed to a preached word that speaks to their hurts and are not being affirmed by their spiritual leaders or their congregations concerning their abusive experiences; therefore, making this research project imperative.

Transformational preaching can serve as a stimulus to lead congregations to begin to have these difficult discussions and acknowledge that the church and pulpit have been silent for too long, and it is time to speak up against these obscenities against women. This research project uses transformational sermons that will incite an action response from the congregation to hear, acknowledge, affirm, and support violated women.

Purpose of the Study

The purpose of this research project is to determine if the use of transformational preaching brings awareness and dismantles the silence in congregations regarding sexual and physical abuse against women, promotes empathy for abused women, and creates a platform to preach, study, and discuss transformative sermons about uncomfortable Scriptures and subjects in the church. In bringing awareness and breaking the silence surrounding all abuse, this research project seeks to address the systemic root of the problem: silence and systematic injustice that replicates itself over and over again in a patriarchally driven society, whose nature is coercive, dismissive, and sexist.

During the study, the congregation experienced a revolutionary awareness of this aberrant yet prevalent violence through transformational preaching. The congregation was also exposed to a different way of hearing Scriptures preached, viewing the Scripture from different hermeneutical lenses, and hearing the voices of the women who have been silenced. Lastly, by acknowledging the need to establish a system that will help transform individuals, the church and the community's approach to hearing and affirming women who have experienced the detrimental effects of physical and sexual abuse changed. Some of these detrimental effects include, but are not limited to, anger, hostility, denial, powerlessness and loss of control, guilt or self-blame, flashbacks, emotional numbness, loss of confidence, mood changes, and embarrassment.

The use of transformative sermons, coupled with group discussions, which include Bible study and prayer, became important instruments in equipping the congregation to break the silence and bring awareness and become responsive to the needs of victimized women within their congregation. This transformation in awareness and breaking of silence within the congregation encouraged the congregants to strive to be a church after God's own heart, a congregation that hears, sees, and acknowledges abused women without subjecting them to shame or revictimization.

Ministry Community

The research ministry community is the congregation of the Second Baptist Church in Asbury Park, New Jersey. The current pastor of the church is an African-American male in his early thirties. The pastor was very supportive of this research project and

7

was instrumental in helping to promote it and in encouraging members and leaders to attend and participate in it.

The community of Asbury Park is approximately 1. 6 square miles in size. It is densely populated and multi-cultural, with over sixty-five churches of various denominations and religious beliefs in the immediate vicinity of Second Baptist Church. Its demographic contains a majority of African Americans, heavily populated with Hispanic/Latino individuals, and a mixture of Caucasians and other ethnic groups. A contributing factor to violence toward women in Asbury Park and surrounding areas is that Asbury Park has a significant presence of various gangs, gang activities and recruitment, violent crime—primarily shootings, drugs, and homelessness.[10] Joblessness, poverty, and insufficient housing are magnifying factors that contribute to domestic violence issues in many communities.

Although Second Baptist Church is centered among a series of low-income housing developments/apartments called "The Projects," it is very involved in its surrounding community. This church is known for standing up against the injustices that infringe upon the quality of life of its citizens. There are many members in the church that are social justice advocates who have organized, participated in, and led marches and demonstrations on behalf of eliminating the inequality and unfair treatment of its residents. However, this church has not initiated any demonstrations against sexual and physical abuse of women as a social justice infringement.

Speaking specifically to Second Baptist's make-up of female congregants, the majority are represented by a more senior population of women who are sixty-five years of age or older. There are women who are between the ages of forty-five and sixty-four.

---

[10] Females are initiated into gangs by being "jumped in," beaten or gang raped by many male gang members in succession.

There is a low representation of those between the ages of nineteen and forty-four, and the age range from pre-teen to eighteen is very underrepresented. The church membership is generational. Most of the senior women have worshiped at this church since they were little girls and have raised their children there. A few of their grandchildren are in attendance. Members often speak of how the church is tradition-based. They have often recalled not clapping or raising their hands as a response to worship. They were still and quiet.

My covenant team consists of seven individuals, both male and female, who committed to assisting me in every way to help obtain the successful completion of the research study. They dedicated themselves to help maintain the integrity of this study by assuring that the collection and recording of data was timely, assisting in the weekly worship services, distributing pertinent data to the congregation, and offering their insights and professional expertise to assure that I met the necessary deadlines in a timely manner.

Thesis Statement

For this research project, transformative sermons were created that utilized Scriptures that are sensitive to and demonstrative of sexual and physical viciousness against women in the Holy Bible. These sermons were used to dismantle the silence and impact the consciousness of the congregation's willingness to address these issues. The transformation in both the laity and leader's affirmation of and response to women who are victimized by sexual and physical abuses is a result of the sermon series.

Informed by the experience and resultant effects of abuse, violence, and trauma upon women, transformative sermons give power and encouragement to congregations to embrace, empathize with, and impart positive affirmation to women who have

experienced the adverse effects of physical and intimate violations that have wounded them and have been left unspoken and
unaddressed. [11] Such preaching, coupled with revelatory group
discussions, Bible study, and prayer, equip the congregation to be
a community of reconciliation and affirmation, as well as a community that is informed about this issue and no longer silent when
confronted by it.

Definition of Terms

For the express purposes of this study, it is important to define
certain terms used throughout this research project.

Affirm is used to acknowledge that sexual and physical abuse
against women is wrong and that assaults are not their fault. It is
also used to give assurance that the church is listening with love
and without judgment. Most importantly, it is used to assure victims that God loves them.

Bring Awareness means to bring knowledge to or heighten
one's understanding or perception of the severity of sexual and
physical violence against women. It is done with the intention that
awareness will cause a more informed response than before.

Break Silence refers to the church's congregation, both laity
and leaders, speaking out against sexual and physical violence
against women, along with the church no longer being idle in its
response to affirm and assist women who have and are experiencing violent abuses. In addition, leaders will preach and teach
texts that demonstrate violence against women, from the lens of
the victim, to help affirm women who have been victimized and
are quietly sitting in the congregation.

---

[11] West, Traci C. *Wounds of the Spirit: Black Women, Violence, and Resistance Ethics.*
New York and London: New York University Press, 1999.

The following are terms that explain various types of rape. **Rape** is defined as a violent crime involving sexual acts forced on one person by another. Technically it is forced penetration (with any body part or foreign object), including anal, vaginal, or oral intercourse. **Incest** is a type of rape and happens when the two parties (rapist and victim) who are involved in the act are closely related by blood, i.e. parents to children, uncles or aunts to nieces or nephews, etc. The term **molestation** describes sexual acts with children up to the age of eighteen, including touching of private parts, exposure of genitalia, inducement to sexual acts with the molester or other person, coupled with forced compliance through intimidation and threat of bodily harm. **Gang rape** is when a group of people forces a person to have sexual intercourse with several offenders against their will. **Partner/Spousal/Marital Rape** is the last rape term to be explained. It is a sexual act committed without a person's consent and/or against a person's will when the perpetrator is the individual's current partner (married or not), previous partner, or cohabitant.

Transformational Preaching is used throughout this research study. It is preaching that invites the hearer to respond positively to the preached Word of God in a manner that changes their perspectives, actions, attitudes, or previous behaviors toward the topic or issue raised. The alteration is not necessarily limited to an outward manifestation but may also be an internal manifestation of change. The response to the transformative word may be physical, spiritual, mental, and/or emotional.

Limitations and Delimitations

Limitations

There were a few limitations with which I had to contend, mainly time constraints. The space in which this research project had taken place is borrowed space. The worship service was set for one hour and was prior to the church's Bible study. In negotiating availability and space, the pastor agreed to allow me to use the sanctuary for the worship experience and the lower fellowship hall for the focus group discussions. Using the lower fellowship hall caused the pastor to move his Bible study to the sanctuary after the worship service. Therefore, it was imperative to be conscious of the time and respect the pastor's generosity. Also, there were variations in attendance for both the worship service and the group discussions. Fortunately, the variation in attendance was not detrimental to the measuring of data. Another limitation was the availability of clinicians and trained professionals who would be available each week. Fortunately, each week, there was a minimum of two clinicians and awareness agencies in attendance, available to anyone wanting to receive their assistance. Additionally, each week, pamphlets and information about various abuse hotlines, help agencies, and counseling agencies were disseminated, posted, and projected, but were not always taken by attendees.

Delimitations

For this study, the participants are within the congregation of Second Baptist Church, Asbury Park, NJ. Although men can be victims of violent abusive relationships and crimes, this study primarily addresses breaking the silence and heightening the awareness of the congregation in response to women who have experienced sexual and physical violence. The sermonic series utilized three scriptures that replicated physical and sexual violence against women. While years can be devoted to this type of research, this research project practicum is four weeks in succession.

Significance of the Study

For far too long, the pulpit has been silent about the issues of sexual abuse, domestic violence, gender relations, and other controversial subjects that are sensitive and uncomfortable to address, especially violence that affects women and children. In this research project, I used transformative sermons to preach to the physical and sexual abuses that affect women, either as those who have been or are still being victimized. In addition, I preached to individuals who have witnessed such abuses while being reared in violent environments. Although there are many programs, shelters, and help aids for women who have had these experiences, for many, the place of worship has not addressed or affirmed these women in a manner that informs them that they:

1. Are not alone;
2. Do not have to be ashamed;
3. Do not need to continue to live in fear;
4. May seek help within their places of worship;
5. Are not forgotten by God;
6. Are loved by God;
7. Are loved by the church; and
8. Have the Word of God as a balm for their healing, hurts, and frustrations.

Christian women who have been violated need to know from the pulpit that their God hears them and has a prophetic and transformative word that affirms them.

Statistically, one in three women, globally, have experienced physical and/or sexual abuse. Sadly, some of these women are sitting in our congregations, looking to hear from their pastors and church leaders a reaffirming word that addresses their experiences and gives them hope in the God they serve, the congregations in which they fellowship, and the pastors who lead them.

A survey conducted of one thousand Protestant pastors, unfortunately, revealed that "the majority of pastors do not consider sexual or domestic violence central to large religious themes such as strong families, a peaceful society, pursuing holiness, social justice, etc. "[12] Additionally,

> "Two out of three (65%) of pastors speak one time a year or less about the issue, twenty-two percent say they speak about it rarely, and one in 10 are silent, never speaking to their congregations about this topic" of sexual and physical abuse. [13]

For too long, pulpits and congregations have been extremely silent and fearful of acknowledging these incursions against women while knowing that these abuses exist and are affecting our congregations. Although there is knowledge of these onslaughts, there is still lack of public awareness that this topic of abuse toward women needs to be addressed in the church, from the pulpit, and within the congregation. Confronting this sin within the worship

---

[12] Assault, South Eastern Center Against Sexual. South Eastern CASA. March 13, 2017. https://www.secasa. com.au/pages/feelings-after-sexual-assault/ (accessed 06 06, 2018).

[13] Assault, South Eastern Center Against Sexual. South Eastern CASA.

service advances the faith community in becoming more reflective of the kingdom God.

Transformational preaching is the major component that other programs and movements have neglected to utilize to bring women who have been traumatized by sexual and physical violence to a place of wholeness within their faith communities. Transformational preaching informs the hearer that God is present and desires a positive change in their lives, not only emotionally and physically but also spiritually. Transformational preaching invites the listener to respond positively to the preached Word of God in a manner that changes their perspectives, actions, attitudes, or previous behaviors toward the topic or issue raised. Transformational preaching converts the faith community, giving it increased awareness and enabling the conscious decision to dismantle the silence within itself by embracing hurting women in their congregation. There are women who blame God and are angry with God because of their harmful experiences, yet, they are in church every Sunday, seeking the presence and embodiment of Jesus within the church leaders and the members they share the Communion table with regularly. During the preaching moment, the Word of God unfolds and expresses the grace and love of God in a manner which they may not have experienced before. Transformational preaching compels believers to respond to God's love and healing in ways that will transform their lives forever.

The focus of this research project is the fullness of God's deity embodied, replicated, and felt in human form through the transformational power of the preached Word of God. This project replicated the ministry of Jesus by bringing a solidarity of humanity and Spirit to the hearers of the Word in a manner that promoted a healthy and inclusive community.

On a global plane, churches, ministries, programs, women, and men will benefit from this research project. The transformational sermons birthed out of this research will be used as a resource to help pastors, clinicians, clergy, and others address violations of women from a biblical perspective, thus allowing them to be integrated into their liturgy, ministry, and counseling environments. This research is a segue for the pulpit pastor and preacher to break the silence on these issues with a bold, transformative word from God during the Sunday morning worship experience. Although speaking out from the pulpit may not end domestic violence and sexual abuse, it will impact the consciousness of the congregation, pierce the silence, and facilitate positive actions to safeguard those who experience abuse.

CHAPTER TWO

Literature Review

Theological

> If we are truly committed to the struggles of our sisters,
> we must forge links with each other whether we are Third
> World women living in Third World countries or Third World
> women trapped in the First World. It is only together that we
> will be able to free our churches and society from the evils
> of race, class, gender and sexual oppression that keep our
> sisters in bondage. [14]

Through a postmodern womanist theology, which emphasizes the significance of wholeness of women, the use of transformational preaching to bring awareness and break the silence in congregations regarding sexual and physical abuse against women was affected through the incorporation of various homiletic and hermeneutic styles. Through the lens and voice of this Black, female preacher who used variations of prophetic, narrative, expository, and incarnational translation, it was effective in bringing awareness of sexual and physical violence against women and its wretchedness to the congregation. Monica A. Coleman's book, *Making a Way Out of No Way: A Womanist Theology*, from

---

[14] Coleman, Monica A. Making a Way Out of No Way: A Womanist Theology. Minneapolis: Fortress Press, 2008.

which the quote above is cited, speaks to the struggles of all women regardless of location. Sexual and physical abuses against women are not limited to color, race, or class; they affect all women globally, as well as the universal Church. Her quote also alludes to the necessity for the church to break the silence regarding sexual and physical abuse against women so that the church is no longer held captive to that silence.

This will also free the church of systemic evils that cripple it as a body, so it may respond in a manner that is an extension of who God is, to replicate the work of Jesus Christ, and embrace the freedom of the Holy Spirit in communities of faith, local communities, and communities globally.

Raquel St. Clair, a womanist theologian, contributes a commentary article entitled, "Womanist Biblical Interpretation" (*True to Our Native Land: An African American New Testament Commentary*). She speaks specifically to African American women and their oppressive experiences with racism, sexism, heterosexism, and classism, and how "womanist symbolizes black women's resistance to their multi-dimensional oppression."[15] However, womanist theology does not only address issues of African American women but those of all women everywhere. However, it hermeneutically gives voice to women through the lens and experiences of "blackness." One of the valuable gems that was gleaned from the article, that was very instrumental in preaching and discussion moments, was the freedom to incorporate my own experience and knowledge of sexual and physical abuse as it relates to the presence of and trust in God. Raquel St. Clair shares in her article how and why Black women who have been abused still show up to church. The most important factor is womanist Christology. When womanist Christology was preached in the sermon series, women

[15] St. Clair, Raquel. "Womanist Biblical Interpretation." True to Our Native Land: An African American New Testament Commentary, 2007: 5–62.

understood and embraced the notion that Black women do not cleave to the suffering of Jesus Christ, but that Jesus cleaves or "binds" Himself to us as we suffer so that we know that we are never alone and God is always with us. Therefore, "womanist Christology, must also affirm black women's faith that Jesus has supported them in their struggles to survive and be free. "[16] This statement was very effective, helpful, and encouraging for both men and women who participated in the group discussions. The importance of God sharing with them helped many to shift from blaming God for difficult life moments to knowing that God has been and still is supporting them through life's trials and tribulations.

In the book, *I Found God in Me: A Womanist Biblical Hermeneutics Reader,* one of the contributors, Katie Geneva Cannon, expounds on how a womanist hermeneutic challenges the normative misogynistic interpretation of Scriptures that negatively depict women in the Scriptures, silencing their voices while diminishing their self-image and self-esteem. She also alludes to the necessity to "elucidate and delegitimize patriarchal teachings" of biblical texts.[17] Throughout the sermon series, while preaching various texts, pastors and leaders were encouraged to explore other lenses and interpretive styles that are more liberating and inclusive of women. Also, these sermons promoted the affirmation of women in the pews week after week and are silently hurting, their anguish not being addressed. Their struggles have been generalized, tossed into the universal struggles of humankind (particularly men), without hearing their unique voice in the Scriptures of the inclusive God. Unfortunately, even when some women preach, their message is drenched in patriarchal idealism, voice, and

---

[16] St. Clair, Raquel. "Womanist Biblical Interpretation." True to Our Native Land: An African American New Testament Commentary, 2007: 54–62.

[17] Smith, Mitzi J., ed. I Found God in Me: A Womanist Biblical Hermenuetics Reader. Eugene: Cascade Books, 2015.

interpretation. *I Found God in Me*, the title of this book, is appropriate for the transformation that has occurred in this researcher–preacher as a result of this research project.

In *God in Her Midst: Preaching Healing to Wounded Women*, Elaine Flake, another womanist theologian, lends her expertise to this project by writing about how the healing and transformative power of the preached Word liberates the minds of hurting women during the worship experience. In addition, through multiple sermons, she explores misjudged women and circumstances in the Holy Scriptures who may be reflected in our congregations. Many African American women attending worship services across the world are broken and seeking the preached Word of God to speak to their hurts, yet the church is silent. Through this resource, I gained a better understanding of how to construct and preach transformative sermons that addressed the hurts of women and revealed the presence of God during their traumatic incidents. I learned that it was essential to present Jehovah-Shammah (God who is there/hears), especially in Judges 19, where God is not mentioned and is seemingly absent. Also, 2 Samuel 13 was preached. During a discussion in the focus group, some mentioned they felt abandoned by God during the worst times of their lives, making it necessary to address this issue, both in discussion and from the pulpit. When addressed in the discussion and during the preached moment, congregants stated how they needed to hear from the pulpit that God is always present because the pulpit is the place of validation for them as the preached word is the Word of God. Additionally, as a result of the transformative sermons preached, the focus group discovered Jehovah-Rapha (God who heals). Even though healing was not the intended goal, this verified the power of God in transformational sermons.

Womanist theologian Traci C. West analyzes the problem of violence against Black women through stories shared by Black women who are survivors of intimate and systemic violence against them, particularly the "historical legacy" of violence against Black women, from slavery to Tina Turner to now, in her book, *Wounds of the Spirit: Black Women, Violence, and Resistance Ethics,* and during a conversation with the author.[18] In this project, systemic violence is attributed to not only racism, sexism, and classism, but to the church. The church itself perpetrates horrible offense against women who have been violently abused by its silence and coercion. Regrettably, the church has been coercive in its demeanor and message. Women are pressured to not respond to or speak of their hurts and violations. Church members have been steamrolled into silence about the atrocities they know take place in the homes of members and within church leadership. There were transformative sermons on biblical texts that demonstrated the power of men's domination silencing and dismissing sexual and physical violations of women. The sermons related to current events that exemplify the same demeanor and biblically described behaviors. These connections uncovered the gross misconduct, for decades, of clergy and church leaders across denominations. The rape of children and women, incidents known by the congregation, the church, and the Pope, are all extremities in which the victims were bludgeoned into silence, ignored, and shut down.

A group of internationally diverse feminist theologians compiled a book of essays entitled *Women Resisting Violence: Spirituality for Life,* about how ethnicity and culture play a significant role in the impact of violence against women worldwide and how to effectively preach to women and congregations with cultural and ethnic differences. In this research study, the congregation is African American, apart from one Caucasian woman, who was also a member of the focus group. For this research project setting, three dominant cultures were discerned and preached

---

[18] Video conference with Dr. Traci West on December 5, 2018.

to, women who have experienced sexual and/or physical abuse, women who have not experienced these abuses, and men. The sermons addressed these various cultures within the congregation simultaneously and cautiously, with care, directness, and information. The sermons, data, and statistics were relatable to each culture, although some may have been recorded by ethnicity, race, classism, and demographic, the commonality being that women were savagely abused. This common denominator was enough for this community to support, affirm, and connect through the transformative preached word.

A relatable and insightful resource is James Nieman and Thomas G. Rogers's book, *Preaching to Every Pew: Cross-Cultural Strategies*. They write, "Ethnicity represents a shared history, one that includes the change and development of a people. "[19] The majority of participants in the focus group shared the same ethnicity but not necessarily the same cultures. *Preaching to Every Pew* helped to distinguish the different variations of cultures within the same ethnicities. This book speaks to the makeup of congregations, their likenesses, similarities, commonalities, and yet, through these differences, the preached moment bridged these differences to create a healthy, diverse, yet inclusive congregation.

Biblical

Transformational sermons are informational and intentional in their purpose and their delivery. Transformative sermons come to life within the preacher and connect to the preacher's knowledge through personal experiences, study of the Scripture narrative, and divine revelation. For such a delicate and important issue, it was imperative to be transparent and relatable without "bleeding"

---

[19] Nieman, James R., and Thomas G. Rogers. Preaching to Every Pew: Cross-Cultural Strategies. Minneapolis: Fortress Press, 2001.

on the congregation. *Mighty Stories, Dangerous Rituals: Weaving Together the Human and the Divine,* by Herbert Anderson and Edward Foley, speaks to "intertwining the divine narrative with human stories" through life experiences.[20] The preached word then becomes reflective of, relatable with, and relevant to the hearer; therefore, the hearer responds to the preached word and desires to engage with it. Based on the sermons preached, the congregations responded with their own stories that helped them cope with various issues and traumatic events in life that related the biblical pericope. Foley and Anderson write:

> The divine narrative tells of God's longing for relationship with ordinary folk. The human narrative records our desires for God and recounts our perennial difficulties in achieving union with the divine. Weaving together human and divine narratives has, as its ultimate goal, the transformation of individual and communal life. [21]

The congregation longs to intertwine the love of God, affirming God's presence in their lives within their individual, personal narratives. Usually, preaching tends to compel individuals to see the presence of God in the everyday well-being of their lives, denying access to those dysfunctional narratives that relate abuse and its barbaric aftermath of silenced voices and lonely confusion. The preponderance of happy preaching negates the need for intervention into dark places by the divine narrative.

When Tamar's history was preached in "Can't You Hear Her?" it required a combination of ideas from *Mighty Stories, Dangerous Rituals*…and hermeneutical and homiletical styles informed by

---

[20] Anderson, Herbert, and Edward Foley. Mighty Stories, Dangerous Rituals: Weaving Together the Human and the Divine. San Francisco: Jossey-Bass, 2001.

[21] Anderson and Foley, 41.

Charles H. Cosgrove and W. Dow Edgerton in their text, *In Other Words: Incarnational Translation for Preaching.*[22] This hermeneutic method creatively explored and preached the tensions between what happened then—Tamar's rape—and the continuous cycle of what is happening now to victims of sexual and physical abuse. A paraphrase of 2 Samuel 13, the narrative of Tamar's rape, was reconstructed to entice the congregation to insert and identify themselves in the story, to recognize their understanding and knowledge or lack thereof, and to bring them to a place of awareness of the pathos of Tamara's plight. This also serves to make them uncomfortable in the comfortable place of silence. Its immediacy provokes them into transformation and action, propelling the congregation to confront the violence and embrace the injured in a manner that extends the healing power and love of God and dispels all feeling of being silenced, rejected, and unheard.

The sermon was dually constructed; its translation was rewritten in today's actual life rhetoric, and then a dramatization of the narrative was created. This "Bibliodrama," a modernized embodied enactment of the biblical narrative, drew the congregation into the experience of a brutal and unsuspected attack that robbed a trusting young woman of her innocence by someone she knew well, trusted, loved, and who, she believed, had an undefiled love for her.[23] This dramatization allowed the congregation to connect with and empathize with the victim, and further, all those who have been victimized, those who are sitting silent, segregated and silenced within the congregation.

Incarnation preaching puts flesh on the Word of God, making the Word become alive in the body of the preacher. "God embraces the human body by the divine Word becoming a body," which

---

[22] Cosgrove, Charles H. and W. Dow Edgerton. In Other Words: Incarnational Translation for Preaching. Grand Rapids: William B. Eerdmans, 2007.

[23] See Appendix, page 172.

reminds us that Jesus, the Word incarnate, became flesh and dwelt among us.[24] Sally A. Brown and Luke A. Powery, in *Ways of the Word: Learning to Preach for Your Time and Place*, speak to the importance of embodying the sermon during the preaching moment. This embodiment creates an atmosphere for a transformational encounter with the living God.

As I recall the transformative sermon that was instrumental in my personal healing journey, it was Dr. Claudette Copeland's embodiment of that sermon that made it dynamic and powerful in the Spirit so I could experience a transformational encounter with the living God. In my preaching, I intentionally embraced and embodied each sermon to effectively engage the congregation with vigor so that others might have the same kind of translating encounter with the living God who transformed my life. Sally Brown, a preaching professor, writes that "A good sermon takes you to a destination worth getting to—an insight, a shift of perspective, some strengthened resolve—and it leads you there by a path you can follow."[25] Although I intentionally embodied each sermon, I was unprepared for the fullness of the destination achieved by both the congregation and myself; the shift in the perspective of the congregation's understanding of the scriptural text, the profound revelation of the seriousness of sexual and physical violence being addressed in the church, and the importance of affirming women who have been maltreated was monumental.

Pamela Cooper-White, a practical theologian, author of *The Cry of Tamar: Violence Against Women and the Church's Responses*, speaks on gender injustice in churches in America. Specifically, she challenges the church to theologically address the severity of violence against women and speaks to the church's failure to do so.

---

[24] Brown, Sally A. and Luke A. Powery. Ways of the Word: Learning to Preach for Your Time and Place. Minneapolis: Fortress Press, 2016.

[25] Brown and Powery, 151.

In this second edition, she measures the progress of the church's response in addressing the issue of domestic and sexual violence in the church and community at large. She notes that the church is still failing miserably in their response to this serious issue.

Brilliantly, Cooper-White introduces the biblical story of Tamar from the perspective of Tamar's niece, Absalom's daughter. As she recounts the story of Tamar's rape, the community of gossiping women also tells the story from their perspective. Cooper-White looks at the community's lack of faith and compassion. She implies that things may have been different if Tamar had

> ...a community of faith to speak a liberating word of hope to her. Faith tells us that what happened to Tamar was a violation, not of her father's property rights and political assets, but a violation of her own personhood. Faith tells us that Tamar did not deserve what happened to her. It was wrong, and it should never have happened. [26]

During the preaching moment, it was vital that these affirmations be stated from the pulpit each week. These faith affirmations were not only indispensable for the congregation to hear in the context of God's Word, but they were especially moving for those who have experienced violent abuses. Also essential was the confirmation of our faith that God did not cause Tamar to suffer. Even though God seemed quiet, God was suffering with Tamar.[27] Comments concerning the validation of women and impressing upon them during the preached moment and during the group discussion that women were not being punished and or abandoned by God was powerfully effective.

---

[26] Cooper-White, Pamela. The Cry of Tamar: Violence against Women and the Church's Response. Second Edition. Minneapolis: Fortress Press, 2012.

[27] Cooper-White, 63.

Cooper-White's incarnational translation of the narrative of Tamar's rape in the voice of Tamar's niece inspired the sermon, "Can't You Hear Her?" The sermon was created and preached in the voice and experience of Tamar herself and the many voices of victims of many ethnicities. It demonstrated the deplorable experience of rape shared among women globally, particularly rape by someone they know. The congregation was disturbed, infuriated, challenged, and empathetic to the appalling violations against women. This sermon also provided leadership with a way to bring justice and empowerment to Tamar and women in the congregation while restoring the relationship of the pulpit and the pew through the transformative preached word.

Haddon W. Robinson's third edition of *Biblical Preaching: The Development and Delivery of Expository Messages* was instrumental in the methodical and focused composition of the Judges 19:22–26 sermon, "The Absence of the Presence of God. " One very important aspect of his methodology of sermon formation greatly influenced and kept me true to the exegesis of the text. Robinson simply asks, "What's the Big Idea?"[28] This simple question assured the sermon to be integral, effective, and transformative. This sermon uncovered the reason for such intemperate attacks and misogynous attitudes displayed throughout the Judges 19 pericope. "The Big Idea" is the systemic evils embedded in the heart of a patristic society. Initially, after this sermon was preached, the feeling of betraying these women was overwhelming. Believing that the story of these women was overlooked and not told was disheartening until the thought of the "The Big Idea" maintained the integrity of the interpretation. The women's story, beyond the rape, is the systemic evil that controlled the rape. The absence of God in the Scripture directly relates to the absence of God in the

---

[28] Robinson, Haddon W. Biblical Preaching: The Development and Delivery of Expository Messages, Third Edition. Grand Rapids: Baker Academic, 2014.

heart of the violators, not just the rapists, but also the fathers, and the Levite.

Marvin A. McMickle's book, *Where Have All the Prophets Gone? Reclaiming Prophetic Preaching in America,* recalls historical prophets as he writes, "The prophets preached truth to power."[29] He continues to speak of the need for prophetic preaching that will communicate in a manner that shifts the focus off the individuals, i.e. , churches and persons, to the realization of the pandemic atrocities in today's societies globally that are not being addressed. McMickle speaks of the necessity of prophetic preaching and its proper perspective. He gives examples of the inappropriate uses of prophetic preaching that damages the people of God instead of uplifting and transforming them and their circumstances through a change of heart, mind, and action.

He issues a call to preachers to return to prophetic sermons that cause congregants to respond to issues greater than the congregation to make a difference in the community and the greater world. It also reminds preachers what prophetic preaching is and why it is needed today. In conjunction, there is Michael Dyson's radical approach to prophetic preaching and his intentionality that incites change. In his book, entitled *Tears We Cannot Stop: A Sermon to White America,* he is intentional in his message, not only to the oppressor but the oppressed in America and worldwide, to make a change in their perspective, reality, and response to the injustices presented through the preached word. He also lends a resolution, in the form of a call to action for both the oppressed and the oppressor alike, as a response to the preached word.

Through their examples of boldness, the prophetic sermon, "The Time Is Now," preached from Isaiah 61:1–3, was birthed; the call to speak truth to power and send out the clarion call to alert

---

[29] McMickle, Marvin A. Where Have All the Prophets Gone? Reclaiming Prophetic Preaching in America. Cleveland: The Pilgrim Press, 2006.

the church that it can no longer sit idly by while social injustices are running rampant and unaddressed. A pastoral study survey polled 1,000 Protestant pastors. Many of these Protestant pastors do not consider sexual and domestic violence to be a central topic to be preached. "Two out of three (65%) pastors speak one time a year or less about the issue. Twenty-two percent say they speak about it once a year. Thirty-three percent of pastors speak about it 'rarely.' And one in 10 are silent, never speaking to their congregations about this topic. They believe the large central topics to be preached are 'strong families, peaceful society, pursuing holiness, and social justice. '"[30] This was very interesting because sexual and domestic violence is connected to each of these issues. My questions to the congregation and leaders were: Is the *family strong* if domestic violence is in the household? Is the *society peaceful* when women are being raped? In *pursuing holiness*, is it supposed to be without wholeness? Is not this issue of sexual and physical abuse an injustice that affects the *social thread* of our society? Preaching a prophetic sermon was essential to this project. The issue of sexual and physical violence against women is a social justice issue that has not taken its rightful place as a societal priority, and it will not if the prophetic voice is not heard from the pulpit and supported by the church.

Ministerial

Sexual and physical abuse is a diabolical and inhumane violation of women that has existed for centuries. Toinette M. Eugene and James Newton Poling stipulated in their book, *Balm in Gilead: Pastoral Care for African American Families Experiencing Abuse*,

---

[30] Sojourners, IMA World Health and. *IMA World Health.* June 2014. https://imaworld-health.org/wp-content/uploads/2014/07/PastorsSurveyReport_final1. pdf (accessed December 17, 2018).

"Racism is the genesis of systematic abuse and oppression in African American families."[31] Although rape is a plague that affects all countries, ethnicities, and classes of women, patriarchy lined with misogyny are additional roots of systemic evils. However, Eugene and Poling continue to expound that

> The wholesale destruction of the black family began during slavery. Whites, in order to maintain the slave system and to justify their inhuman treatment of blacks, developed a vicious mythology to support their actions. To the detriment of all society, this mythology persists to this day. White people based their barbaric system of supremacy, domination, and control on the belief that all black people were insatiable sexual beasts.[32]

Collectively, the statistical rate of Black women raped and assaulted is significantly higher than any other race of women.

1. African Americans
   - An estimated 29. 1 percent of African-American females are victimized by intimate partner violence in their lifetime (rape, physical assault, or stalking).
   - African-American females experience intimate partner violence at a 35 percent higher rate than that of White females, and about two and a half times the rate of women of other races. However, they are less likely than White women to use social services, battered women's programs, or go to the hospital because of domestic violence.

---

[31] Eugene, Toinette M., and James Newton Poling. *Balm For Gilead: Pastoral Care for African American Families Experiencing Abuse*. Nashville: Abingdon Press, 1998.

[32] Eugene and Poling.

- According to the National Violence Against Women Survey (NVAWS). African American women experience higher rates of intimate partner homicide when compared to their White counterparts.
- Statistics show that African-American women typically comprise about 70 percent of Black congregations. Religious convictions and a fear of shame or rejection from the church may contribute to their remaining in an abusive relationships.[33]

2. All women
   - Domestic Violence: A person is abused in the United States every nine seconds (Bureau of Justice Statistics).[34]
   - Sexual Violence: one in four women and one out of six men are sexually abused in their lifetime (Department of Justice).[35]
   - Globally, as many as 38 percent of murders of women are committed by an intimate partner. 200 million women have experienced female genital mutilation/cutting. 35 percent of women worldwide have experienced either physical and/or sexual intimate partner violence or non-partner sexual violence, and globally

---

[33] Women of Color Network. *Women of Color Network.* June 2006. www.doj.state.or.us/wp-content/uploads/2017/08/women_of_color_network_facts_domestic_violence_2006. pdf (accessed January 17, 2019).

[34] Sinozich, Sofi, Lynn Langton, Ph.D. , Bureau of Justice Statistics. Bureau of Justice Statistics. December 11, 2014. http://www.bjs.gov/index.cfm?ty=pbdetail&iid=5176 (accessed August 21, 2018).

[35] The Center for Family Justice: Statistics. n.d. https://centerforfamilyjustice. org (accessed January 17, 2019).

7 percent of women have been sexually assaulted by
someone other than a partner (Department of Justice).[36]

These alarming statistics and others demonstrate the global
pandemic of violence against women. These statistics were used
to bring awareness and educate the congregation and leaders who
may not be conscious that this issue is serious and worldwide and
that these vicious assaults are mounting at a shocking rate.

As stated previously, women who have been severely abused
are silent in the pews, afraid or ashamed to say a word. And truthfully speaking, the congregation is most likely unwilling, not being
informed or trained in how to embrace, engage, and affirm them.
Authors Brenda Branson and Paula Silva, in their book, *Violence
Among Us*, address the issue of bringing awareness to the church
and how to appropriately engage and affirm women in the church
who are currently living in domestic violence situations or have
been victimized by such abuse. The authors' intentions are to equip
the church to respond and minister effectively to families who
experience such hostility and atrocities. With the information
gained in this source, I was able to be intentionally more sensitive to the plight of these women and not react instinctively as
protector or problem solver. The information that was shared and
preached from the pulpit had a three-fold effect. It brought the
people in the congregation to a place where they could respond
appropriately to those who have been victimized, assured them
that the church is a safe place for everyone, and made it common
knowledge that no one is to be violated or touched in a manner
that makes them uncomfortable.

---

[36] Sinozich, Sofi, Lynn Langton, Ph.D. , Bureau of Justice Statistics. Bureau of Justice
Statistics. December 11, 2014. http://www.bjs.gov/index.cfm?ty=pbdetail&iid=5176
(accessed August 21, 2018)

In their research posted by the National Online Resource Center on Violence Against Women, Carolyn M. West and Kalimah Johnson include variables to consider when measuring the responses of those who have been sexual abused. Although abused people may share the same ethnicity, the place, timing of the event in life, their social status, social involvements, who the abuser is, and place of abuse must be taken into consideration when weighing their responses.

Additionally, their research entitled, "Sexual Violence in the Lives of African American Women," gives insights into culturally sensitive techniques that increase personal resilience while dismantling the myth of African-American women being "strong Black women."[37] This source, coupled with the article, "The Lived Experience with Christianity and Teenage African-American Females' Perceptions of Their Self-Esteem," by Daphne King explores the journey of several African-American teen girls, ages sixteen to eighteen, who incorporate their daily experiences, faith, and prayer lives to enhance their self-esteem. The issue of self-esteem and the myth of always having to be a "strong Black woman" were central topics in group discussions. There were individuals who were strengthened by the preached word. It gave them the courage to address personal issues and allowed them to open up and address issues of being tired of being the "strong Black woman" in their fragile state. Some of the women appeared to have gained more confidence to be verbal about their struggles with self-esteem, sharing, and encouraging one another and themselves. Processing the preached word, particularly sermons and affirmations that confirmed the love and presence of God, gave them weekly strength and encouragement. It appeared that many

---

[37] West, Carolyn M. and Kalima Johnson. "National Online Resource Center on Violence Against Women." *VAWnet.org*. March 2013. https://vawnet.org/sites/default/files/materials/files/2016-09/AR_SVAAWomenRevised. pdf (accessed November 23, 2018).

in the focus group not only gained awareness of the issue but, more importantly, gained awareness of themselves.

In his book, *(Un)Qualified: How God Uses Broken People to Do Big Things*, author Steven Furtick speaks about how God accepts all people as they are. He speaks from personal experience of not feeling qualified to be used by God, particularly in ministry. He tries to teach the reader how to allow one to see as God sees, and to close one's eyes to how the enemy manipulates one to see oneself as less. Furtick writes, "We must embrace who we are before we can become who we were meant to be. "[38] Although we may have endured hardships, have been violated, or have violated others, Furtick helps us to realize that God loves us just as we are. If we are to grow, we must own that person whom God sees; we must be true to ourselves just as we are. We must own the effects of traumatic situations in our lives so that those events and the stigma that accompanies them no longer have the power to be crippling, distracting, or disabling. He continues: "God cannot bless who we pretend to be. "[39] This is not a derogatory statement or one that would imply that women are pretending to have been hurt or violated. This statement, for me, speaks to the silence that denies physical and sexual violations suffered by women. This book is an encouragement for women to acknowledge the impact of the violation and an invitation to be free to be who God created them to be, even with the blemishes and scars they have covered for so long. Mostly, this book was a guide to ensure that the women were affirmed regularly and constantly reminded that God loves us all just the way we were created and according to design, "before the

---

[38] Furtick, Steven. *(Un)Qaulified How God Uses Broken People To Do Big Things.* Colorado Springs: Multnomah Books, 2013.

[39] Furtick, page 11.

foundations of the world. "[40] Therefore, each person is to allow himself/herself to be seen as God sees him/her and not how the enemy manipulates him/her into seeing himself/herself as less.

Christie Cozad Neuger's *Counseling Women: A Narrative, Pastoral Approach*, offers a new radical feminist approach to counseling women who experience sexism and are hurt by our patriarchal society. Neuger offers a concise methodical structure for counseling and empowering women who have been plagued by violent life events, a structure that is efficient and therapeutic. Her methods are effective for laypeople engaging in pastoral care that are not professional clinicians, and so they assisted in the formatting and shaping of the group discussions in this study. Her approach led to empowering women to regain their confidence and strength in a setting that was previously not aware of or sensitive to their experiences as injured women. Among the objectives of transformational preaching are restoring women's voices, hearing their plights, strengthening them, and empowering them to empower other women. Incorporating the method shared by Neuger will help this research project attain those goals of transformational preaching.

Lastly, *Listening to Listeners: Homiletical Case Studies*, by John S. McClure, Ronald J. Allen, Dale P. Andrews, L. Susan Bond, Dan P. Moseley, and G. Lee Ramsey, Jr., reminds the preacher to not only preach the sermon but also listen to the sermon as it is being preached; not only listening to oneself, but also, the non-verbal communication spoken by the congregation as they are hearing and experiencing the sermon. In doing so, transformational

---

[40] Ephesians 1:4.

preaching will have qualities that bring about a "change in heart and mind. "[41]

This book contains interviews with various congregants from diverse congregations who share how they perceive and respond to the preached word. The interviews in this book helped inform this preacher on how to listen to the focus group as they interpreted their encounters with the sermons preached during this research project.

Within the study's interviews, some congregants also shared how they appreciated a time of reflection and engaging in dialogue about the sermon after the church service, downstairs in fellowship. Additionally, the information concerning the expectations of the congregants helped inform the shaping and delivery of the sermons. Lastly, the book underscored *the importance of listening*, encouraging the preacher to listen to the interviewed congregants' spoken and unspoken language, and continuing to learn how to listen to parishioners. The atmosphere created for the focus group was one that was comfortable and welcoming. There was coffee and tea, and light refreshments were served weekly. These surroundings relaxed the participants so that they could engage in meaningful conversation. As they spoke, they felt like a family and were grateful to have each other, as was I grateful to have each of them.

---

[41] McClure, John S., Ronald J. Allen, Dale P. Andrews, L. Susan Bond, Dan P. Moseley, and G. Lee Ramsey, Jr. *Listening to Listeners: Homiletical CASE STUDIES.* St. Louis: Chalice Press, 2004.

CHAPTER THREE

Methodology

This research project was instituted at the Second Baptist Church in Asbury Park, New Jersey, for four weeks, beginning on February 6, 2019. The project would determine if the use of transformational preaching in this congregation would bring awareness and break the silence concerning physical and sexual abuse against women. To have an authentic worship and preaching experience as close to a Sunday morning worship experience as possible, Wednesday nights were selected to have the worship experience, entitled "Hour of Power," followed by one-hour focus group discussions. The worship experiences were for one hour prior to the church's Bible study, as the pastor and I agreed, so as not to interfere with regular church activities. A series of four transformative sermons were preached, one each week. The "Hour of Power" worship services were open to the public and not limited to the congregation at Second Baptist Church.

The sermons, worship services, and focus groups were strategically formulated to obtain maximum outcome of this research project's objectives:

- To circulate crucial information about sexual and physical violence against women;
- To introduce local agencies and counselors that support, aid, and assist victimized women;

- To introduce and preach violent biblical texts and subject matter that have been taboo in the church and are not preached from the voice of the violated. Also, to address societal and systemic evils, such as patriarchy, sexism, White supremacy and privilege, classism, and racism.[42]
- To create space for the focus group to process and discuss the information preached, ask questions, and comment on the preached message and the sermons' effectiveness based on their personal understanding of and engagement with the text; and
- To create a church community that affirms and extends God's love to women who may have experienced or may still be experiencing physical and sexual abuse.
- Three-and-a-half weeks before the dissertation sermon series began, there was a video appeal and weekly spoken and printed advertisements to introduce and announce the research project to solicit the congregation's participation and support and promote the project's purpose and importance. [43] These methods were very effective; however, the congregation was slow in responding. They appeared to need more information. Therefore, each week during the announcements, they were given more information based on the questions I received after each previous Sunday morning's announcement. There was a misunderstanding about the criteria of who could participate. One concern expressed was whether men were invited to attend the services and if they could participate in the focus group. Another concern for many women was that they initially thought they had to know or have known someone or were

---

[42] Sermons are listed in Appendix F, Pages 161 ff.

[43] https://youtu.be/o26I1uVJif0.

themselves currently experiencing a form of sexual and physical abuse. Once these concerns were addressed, the congregation quickly responded to the call to participate. The entire congregation was encouraged to attend the dissertation sermon series without having to commit to participating in the surveys.

Surveys

Forty persons, both men and women, agreed to participate in the research project surveys, (of which approximately 80 percent actually participated: twenty-three women and nine men).[44] Of the forty, ten were leaders, either clergy, deacons, or deaconesses (also, 80 percent participated, two women and six men). Out of the forty, a focus group of fifteen was created, comprised of both laity and leaders, men and women (86 percent consistently participated, two men and eleven women), to discuss the effectiveness of the sermons, their understanding of the sermons, and the relativity of the sermon on the issue of sexual or physical abuse against women. To generate data to evaluate the effectiveness of transformational sermons to bring awareness and break the silence in congregations concerning sexual and physical abuse against women, surveys were constructed using a quantitative approach in the form of a Likert scale. [45] To maintain anonymity, each participant received a number on a folded paper drawn out of a bag and was asked to remember this number as his or her identifier when filling out the surveys. They were each instructed to record or take a picture of the number on their phone or put the paper in their wallets

---

[44] See Appendix D pages 125 ff for samples of each survey utilized.

[45] A survey scale represents a set of answer options—either numeric or verbal—that cover a range of opinions on a topic. It uses question that presents respondents with pre-populated answer choices.

or purses to help ensure accuracy in tracking the data received from each person. The numbers for the laity were from 001 through 030, and the numbers for the leaders were from 200 through 210. Although everyone's anonymity would be maintained throughout the study, each leader and focus group volunteer signed a consent to participate form. The Consent Form to Participate in Research Study identifies the researcher, her faculty advisor and e-mail information, the educational institution, the procedure, potential benefits and risks of their participation, and the confidentiality of any information to be disclosed only with their permission as required by law.[46] Lastly, the participants were informed that, in accordance with the guidelines of New Brunswick Theological Seminary, all information discussed, documented, and gathered to assist in evaluating the desired goals of the research project will be kept safely.

The first surveys created, issued, and answered by the forty volunteers were a pre-project congregational survey and a pre-project leadership survey. The congregation's pre-project survey was distributed and collected prior to the start of the dissertation sermon series. The pre-project survey was used to establish a baseline to determine the level of awareness and willingness to dismantle the silence of sexual and physical abuses of women within the ecclesiastical community. The leaders' pre-project survey was distributed prior to the initial preaching of the dissertation sermon series. The leaders' pre-project survey was used to establish a baseline to determine many variables, such as:

- What is the likelihood that leaders will preach and/or teach those violent Scriptures that illustrate sexual and physical abuses of women while addressing the issue of the abuse?

---

[46] Consent to Participate form is located in Appendix E pages 153 ff.

- What is each one's perceived level of influence on the congregation?
- How do they, as significant church leaders, envision their role in affirming women who have been traumatized by abuse?
- How aware and familiar are leaders with reporting procedures and community resources that support victims of sexual and physical abuse?
- How comfortable are they with initiating discussions about the importance of addressing sexual and physical violence against women with other ecclesiastical leaders?

The next two surveys were a weekly congregational survey and a weekly focus group survey, distributed to all forty volunteers for each of the four weeks. Eight of the questions in each survey were identical; the focus group surveys had two additional questions focusing on that group's sessions. These surveys were used to measure the effectiveness of transformative sermons to increase the congregation's knowledge of the biblical accounts of assaults against women and their relevance in connection with the current era's pandemic of violence against women. The survey questioned the effectiveness, educational value, and relevance of the sermon, along with its value in prompting listeners to action, as well as the effectiveness of the sermon in spurring the small-group discussion.

Concluding the sermon series, two more surveys were formulated: a post-project congregational survey and a post-survey leadership survey. These surveys were used to measure the shift in the understanding and knowledge of sexual and physical violence against women, the perceived need to discuss, teach, and preach this vital issue within the church, and any increase in empathy or affirmation of women who have been or still are being sexually or physically abused.

All the survey questions were informed by surveys conducted by IMA WorldHealth and Sojourners: Faith in Action for Social Justice, and the Science, Religion, and Culture Program at Harvard Divinity School. [47, 48]

Worship Service and Sermons

Each Wednesday evening for four consecutive weeks, except for one service rescheduled due to hazardous weather conditions, there was a worship experience (church service) entitled, "Hour of Power," from 6 pm to 7 pm. The orders of worship for these services were strategically devised to closely resemble the church's Sunday morning order of service. While the sermons were preached from the pulpit, I felt it necessary to create an atmosphere with the authenticity of a Sunday morning service. The order of service included the call to worship, invocation, praise and worship period, Scripture readings, welcome/statement of purpose, song selections, sermon, prayer, offering, and the benediction.[49]

It was not only necessary to create an atmosphere of worship, but to also create an innocuous atmosphere for anyone who might be in attendance who may be experiencing or have experienced physical and or intimate abuse. It was important to inform those who have experienced or are experiencing abuse that there were safeguards in place should they need to speak to someone. During

---

[47] Sojourners, IMA World Health and. *IMA World Health.* June 2014. https://imaworld-health.org/wp-content/uploads/2014/07/PastorsSurveyReport_final1. pdf (accessed December 17, 2018).

[48] Science, Religion, and Culture Harvard Divinity School. *Interrogating the Silence: Religious Leaders' Attitudes towards Sexual and Gender-based Violence.* Final, Harvard Divinity School, Cambridge: Harvard Divinity School, 2015.

[49] See Appendix F, pages 162 ff. Order of service examples are attached to each sermon respectively.

each service, licensed clinicians, counselors, and representatives from various local agencies were present and available to assist women who had experienced or were continuing to experience domestic violence or rape. An announcement was made each week identifying the various help agency representatives and the safe rooms provided for anyone who needed to speak to someone privately and confidentially.[50] Anyone needing to take advantage of the safe rooms was instructed to self-identify to the clinician upon entering the designated safe room. Also, the names of various emergency help centers, hotlines, and telephone numbers were included in the weekly verbal announcements and displayed on the video monitors. Each person was encouraged to write down the numbers to share with others. In addition, postcards were created and distributed with same emergency numbers that were displayed on the video monitors. A plethora of user-friendly help agencies' advertisements and awareness pamphlets were strategically and conveniently placed within the upper and lower sanctuaries for anyone to take voluntarily. Having these resources readily available was essential, considering the emotionally tricky yet violent nature of this issue. During this project, many of these agencies made known their desire to partner with the church around the issues of sexual and physical abuse.

Immediately following the worship experience, the focus group reconvened in the lower sanctuary from 7:00 pm to 8:00 pm. I provided refreshments to help establish a comfortable and relaxing atmosphere for discussions and critiques of the sermons and worship experiences. The discussions of the focus group were recorded and later transcribed for the purpose of recalling pertinent information for use in the study. The transcriber was given the Consent Form to Participate in Research Study to sign that

---

[50] Safe rooms are three rooms that were set aside for private, one-on-one consultations with clinicians apart from both the upper and lower sanctuaries.

indicated her willingness to participate in the study and stipulated the necessity of professionalism and confidentiality.[51]

The Scriptures and Sermons

The scriptural texts were deliberately chosen for this series of transformative sermons. The sermons explored problematic, challenging, and controversial Scriptures containing violent abuses against women from a deliberately non-patriarchal perspective. These transformative sermons informed the congregation about the universal evils that are at the root of and uphold sexual and physical violence against women. These systemic issues include but are not limited to patriarchy, classism, White supremacy and privilege, sexism, racism, and political privilege and corruption. The sermons were approximately twenty minutes in length and used various hermeneutic and homiletical styles of prophetic, incarnational translation, narrative, and expository. The scriptural texts and sermon titles were:

- Isaiah 61:1–3, "The Time Is Now." This scripture is thematic for the research project. The sermon introduced the dissertation project and theme. It addressed stories of sexual and physical abuse of women in the Holy Bible, the role of patriarchy, and the silencing of women who were horribly violated. This sermon began with disturbing national and global statistics concerning sexual and physical abuse against women. It concluded with a prophetic clarion call to clergy and congregations to break the silence surrounding sexual and physical abuses against women, insisting that this is the acceptable year of the Lord, and the

---

[51] See Appendix E, page 153 for consent form for transcriber.

time is now for the church to join in the fight to dismantle the plague of abuse against women.

• 2 Samuel 13, "Can't You Hear Her?" This sermon addressed the atrocious rape of Tamar by her half-brother Amnon with a twist. A twenty-first century version of the pericope was created using incarnational translation. A combination of preaching and role-play brought Tamar to life to deconstruct the silence of victims and the actions to "protect them" while leaving victims displaced, disgraced, and isolated.

• Judges 19:22–26, "The Absence of the Presence of God. " This sermon treated the violence against the unnamed concubine and the willingness of a father to sacrifice his virgin daughters in a land that had no king, where everyone did what was right in their own sight. In this land, the hearts of the people lacked the presence of God. This sermon expounded on how both then and now, "men of God," priests, pastors, deacons, and other clergies who are operating in revered positions suffer from the absence of the presence of God in their hearts.

• Genesis 34, "What's Love Got to Do with It?" This narrative sermon explored the story of Dinah, the rape and the actions of the men who supposedly loved her. Dinah is betrayed by each of them: her father, her brothers, and the rapist by means of manipulation, coercion, and sexism. All these men misused, abused, and contorted the true meaning of love. Just like Dinah, many women have been seduced by a disfigured representation of love. God is the perfect example of love, and through this sermon, we helped redefine love for some, affirm others, and as an instrument of God, give love.

- Each of these sermons addressed systemic issues that were prevalent in the Old Testament and are still infecting and negatively influencing society today.

CHAPTER FOUR

Implementation of the Project

The spirit of the Lord God is upon me, because the Lord
has anointed me; he has sent me to bring good news to the
oppressed, to bind up the brokenhearted, to proclaim liberty to the captives, and release to the prisoners; *to proclaim
the year of the Lord's favor,* and the day of vengeance of our
God; to comfort all who mourn; to provide for those who
mourn in Zion—to give them a garland instead of ashes, the
oil of gladness instead of mourning, the mantle of praise
instead of a faint spirit. They will be called oaks of righteousness, the planting of the Lord, to display his glory.[52]

This research project was instituted in the main sanctuary
at the Second Baptist Church in Asbury Park, New Jersey,
beginning on February 6, 2019, to determine if the use of transformational preaching would bring awareness and break the silence
in congregations concerning physical and sexual abuse against
women. Three-and-a-half weeks prior to beginning the dissertation sermon series, there was a video appeal and weekly verbal-
ized and printed advertisements to introduce and announce the
research project at the church, to solicit the congregation's participation and support, and to promote the research project's purpose

---

[52] Isaiah 61:1–3; emphasis mine.

and importance. The pastor was very supportive of this researcher and research project and was instrumental in helping to promote this research project and in encouraging members and leaders to attend and participate in the research study. Additionally, the pastor also made it possible to have the project announced at the Seacoast Missionary Baptist Association's Installation of Officers service. [53] At this service, the pastor proudly introduced the candidate and allowed the candidate to introduce the research project and invite those assembled to attend the worship experience to support the research project and the candidate in her efforts.

There were several sexual abuse and domestic violence emergency help agencies and organizations that were solicited to attend and provide pamphlet information—and clandestine services, if necessary—to anyone who may seek their assistance during and after the services. The pamphlets and fliers were distributed and strategically placed in the main sanctuary and lower sanctuary of the church weekly. Some of the agency representatives and counselors who attended weekly were Displaced Homemakers Service; Mercy Center: A Community Victim Witness Advocacy Program; 180 Turning Lives Around, Inc. ; Jackson Counseling Services; and an independent licensed clinical social worker. Each week, there were at least two clinicians in attendance to provide services, if needed. Additional agencies provided informational pamphlets for distribution and display but were not able to attend were Providence House (Ocean County), the National Domestic Violence, Mental Health Services in Monmouth County, New Jersey State Bar Foundation New Jersey Law Center, Parents Anonymous of New Jersey, Inc. , No Means No: Information for Teens, and New Jersey Department of Children and Families.

---

[53] The Seacoast Baptist Association is a conference of numerous Baptist churches within Monmouth and Ocean Counties. This is the association with which our church is affiliated.

Some of the information supplied was also in Spanish. A few of the help agency representatives and counselors who attended the weekly services were Spanish-speaking. Some of the help agencies expressed their desire to connect or partner with churches concerning sexual and domestic violence and were excited to attend this type of service in the church.

The worship service was advantageously planned and structured to coordinate with the minister of music and the AV ministry for maximum effectiveness. Each was provided with an Order of Service weekly for optimal effect of the visual display of the biblical Scriptures in the New Revised Standard translation on the sanctuary screens.[54] In addition, prior to the congregation's arrival, the image designed specifically for this research project was displayed on the screen, welcoming them to the "Hour of Power" worship experience. The minister of music also played recorded music while attendees arrived. The minister of music chose musical selections that were appropriate to enhance the worship service, invoke the presence of the Holy Spirit, and accompany the scriptural text. Some of the musical selections were at my request to help enhance the effectiveness of the transformative sermon preached. The general Order of Service included:

- Call to Worship and Invocation
- Praise and Worship Selection(s)
- Welcome and Statement of Purpose: During this time, the attendees were welcomed and thanked for attending the service; an explanation of the intention of the research project was stated; instructions for the distribution, filling out, and submission of surveys were given. A reminder for the focus group to reconvene in the lower sanctuary

---

[54] See Appendix F pages 161 ff for each Order of Service; they are presented with their respective sermons.

was given. The clinicians and agency representatives were identified as well as the "safe rooms" for private discussions. Emergency hotline and agency numbers were displayed during this portion of the service, and the congregation was encouraged to write down or take a photo of the image displayed. The importance of not being ashamed to seek counseling services was stressed, and any other pertinent information or announcements was shared.

- Scripture Reading(s)
- Musical Selection
- Sermon (approximately twenty minutes in duration)
- Altar call or Prayer
- Offering
- Benediction

Each participant was asked and notified prior to the beginning of services. The inclusion of congregants on the program helped the congregation to own the experience and importance of the project. They all did well and were glad to be asked and enthused to be a part of "this important work."[55]

Sexual and physical violence against women is a serious issue that needs to be taken seriously. To preach these issues, the sermons must be transformative and intentional, as well as the preacher. It was important to not only be deliberate in the delivery but also in appearance. The internationally identified color for sexual violence is teal, and the color for domestic (physical) violence is purple. Intentionally, for the first and last night of "Hour of Power," I wore a purple clerical shirt with a royal blue robe (I do not own a teal robe yet) and purple stilettos. It was very important to wear the colors, clergy robe, collar, and stilettos as a woman preacher. It demonstrated that I am called by and operating under

---

[55] "This important work" is the phrase used by many to describe this research project.

the authority of God, and I have been appointed for this specific task. Additionally, it stated that I believe in and identify with what I am preaching and supporting, and I am a woman unashamed. Lastly, the wearing of the colors informed the congregation of the meaning of each color, promoted the cause, and the necessity to bring awareness and break the silence of sexual and physical violence against women.

Pre and Post Surveys

This sermon also addressed some concerns discovered in the responses to the pre-survey questionnaire by the congregation (which includes the leadership as well). Thirty-two pre-survey questionnaires were filled out and turned in, which is 80 percent of the sample population. Of the thirty-two, 25 percent were men and 75 percent were women. The questions that had responses that concerned me were numbers eight, "Those who have experienced a form of sexual or physical abuse should remain silent and get over it," and ten, "I believe the Holy Scriptures (the Bible) supports violence against women." For question eight, one person responded with *strongly agree*, and two persons indicated that they agree that women who have experienced a form of sexual or physical abuse should remain silent and get over it. Although the response to this question is only .09 percent, it needed to be addressed through the preached word and supported with statistical data.

The responses for the weekly congregation and focus group questions were the following:

- Totally reflects/is relevant (Excellent)
- Embraces most of the text (Good)
- Somewhat (Fair) or
- Does not reflect/not relevant (Poor)

When expressing the statistical results of the data for all weekly congregation and focus group, the results of *Excellent* or *Good* were combined to derive the percentage. Both responses indicate the effectiveness and or understanding of the questions asked to the individuals, therefore, giving an accurate statistical analysis for informational purposes.

Interestingly, only twenty-one post-survey questionnaires were filled out and submitted, which is only 52 percent of the sample population. Of the twenty-one who submitted their surveys, 10 percent were men and 90 percent were women. However, in the post-survey questionnaire, each of them changed their position to *strongly disagree.* Their responses to the pre and post surveys were tracked by the number identifier each person drew prior to filling out the pre-surveys. Oddly, there was one answer to this question on the post-survey that strongly agreed but had initially strongly disagreed, most likely, this person was rushing and misread the question or the responses. As to the second question that raised concern—number ten—as to their belief that the Scriptures support violence against women, 25 percent of the thirty-two survey takers either strongly agreed or agreed that the Bible supports violence against women. In the post-survey questionnaire, 40 percent of the twenty-one persons still believed that the Holy Scriptures supported violence against women. After evaluating these results, it is understandable how those participants would believe the Bible supports violence against women; however, it is very possible that because the Bible records so many outrageous violations against women, it appears to support the violence as opposed to it being a recording of the violent acts. The concern was to assure that through preaching, the hearers would not confuse the violent acts in the Bible as God condoning the violence against women or as the acts being punishment from God. Perhaps the question could have been worded differently.

During the focus group discussions, this question was discussed in the group in conjunction with the sermon. The intent of the question was clarified, and some had blamed God for the violence and revered it as punishment from God; however, this misunderstanding was addressed and dispelled to insure their understanding that God did not condone or indict such severe punishment upon these women or those who have been and still are victims of abuse. This topic was reiterated and preached in multiple sermons throughout the sermon series.

The pre-congregation survey indicated the congregation believes it is very important for the church to address the issue of sexual and physical violence against women from the pulpit. Additionally, the congregants indicated they believed in the importance of the congregation and leadership to join together for action and advocacy to end the silence around sexual and physical violence against women. They also indicated they were much aware of the pandemic of these abuses; however, the congregants' responses to the questionnaires indicate that they have rarely, if ever, been exposed to sermons that speak to the sexual and physical abuse of women. When the pericopes of Tamar, Dinah, and the unnamed concubine were read and preached, many verbally indicated they had never read or heard of these particular women and their stories. When these events were preached during this series, it was the first time many had heard them preached. Interestingly, in addition to the congregation being much aware of the pandemic of these abuses, they happen to agree that the women who have been victimized are silent and do not seek assistance amongst them because of the disbelief of those surrounding them (the victimized).

Ten pre-survey questions for church leadership were distributed, and eight were filled out and submitted. Out of the 80 percent participation of leadership, six were men and two were women in leadership. About half reported they had either preached or heard sermons related to sexual and physical abuse, while the other half had not. Although half indicated they have not heard or preached sermons on these issues, all of them indicated that they would likely teach or preach on the subject matter in addition to having the desire to attend training to acquire learning tools to equip church leaders to be supportive of women who have been sexually and physically violated. Church leaders also believe in the necessity to affirm violated women, and as leaders, they are affluential in leading the congregation to do so as well. A distressing discovery in this survey is that 75 percent of the leadership encountered couples who were involved in domestic violence. Of that percentage, 37. 5 percent did not alert authorities but instead counseled the couple(s). Fortunately, the other 37. 5 percent advised the victim to leave the relationship. Seventy-five percent of the leadership is aware of the emergency help services that are local in the community, although there was no literature in the church prior to this research project.

Unfortunately, the participation of the leadership was sporadic, although many of those in leadership were in attendance each week and well represented, not all faithfully participated in the surveys. The post-survey questions for leaders marginally maintain the same throughout, except for a decrease in the likelihood to preach those difficult texts and violent abuses. Also, a slight increase in the leadership's knowledge of local emergency help agencies is noticed.

The Scriptures and Sermons

The scriptural texts were deliberately chosen for this series of transformative sermons. The sermons were preached from the perspective and voice of a woman as opposed to the familiar and traditional patriarchal perspective. The sermons explored and exposed those problematic, challenging, and controversial Scriptures pertaining to violent abuses against women. These transformative sermons informed the congregation, through the preached word, about the universal evils that are at the root of and uphold sexual and physical violence against women. These systemic issues include, but are not limited to, patriarchy, classism, White supremacy and privilege, sexism, racism, and political privilege and corruption.

Sermon One

The first sermon in the series was, "The Time Is Now," from the Old Testament Scripture accredited to the prophet Isaiah in Isaiah 61:1–3. This scripture is the thematic scripture for this research project. This prophetic sermon was used to introduce the dissertation project and theme, and to set the stage for the sermon series. This prophetic sermon disrupts the status quo. It called out hypocrisy hiding in plain sight among the people of God. It depicted the edicts delivered to the people of God by the prophets concerning God's displeasure of the leader's lack of compassion for, as well as them not attending to and speaking up for the needs of the oppressed. God upholds the cause of the oppressed, disheartened, abused, and those whose voices have been stifled. This sermon also pointed to where God is directing ministers and leaders. God is calling them to a higher level of preaching, a level in which preachers and teachers must speak directly, naming the root and spirit that has caused certain skewed and tainted thinking in the minds of Christians. Therefore, leaders can no longer approach serious issues with "kid-glove" treatments of topics that must be intentionally and explicitly exposed. This exposure is through the preaching and teaching to the people of God so that the people of God may experience deliverance to fight for and free the oppressed and suffering as a result of these systemic attacks of physical and sexual abuses.

This sermon declared that *the time is now* for the church to spring into action, speak up, and no longer turn a deaf and unknowing ear and attitude toward the alarming issues of sexual and physical violence against women. It addressed sexual and physical abuse of women in the Holy Bible, the role of patriarchy, and the silencing of women who have been sadistically violated. This sermon began with disturbing statistics concerning sexual and physical abuse against women, nationally and globally, as well as the alarming statistical difference of the higher rate African-American women recorded rapes as opposed to White women and women of other races. This particular statistic was important to include for a congregation with approximately a 90 percent attendance rate of African Americans each week.

This sermon also gave disturbing statistics of how, out of 1,000 Protestant pastors, the majority did not believe that sexual and physical violence was central topic or issue to be preached. Instead, they believed centralized and more important topics to be preached were "strong families, peaceful society, pursuing holiness, and social justice. "[56] The sermon also pointed out the issues of sexual and physical violence that are imperative to the achievement of each of these centralized topics. When these abuses are present in the home and in families, then the family is *not* strong. When rape and other variations of sexual assault are at high alarming rates, then society is *not* peaceful. If one is suffering from or committing these violent offenses, then they are *not* whole; therefore, holiness is not attainable. And lastly, the injustice of sexual and physical abuses affect and weaken the social thread of our society. Therefore, social justice is not without the cry for justice for those who have been silenced and injured by sexual and physical violence.

This sermon also spoke to the need to break the silence of these abuses, the need to address the hurts of women in the congregation from the pulpit, and to affirm the abused. Granted, preachers are preaching to various situations and circumstances, yet, are not preaching to the hurt of our women. Women are sitting in the pews, silently screaming, "We are here, we have been hurt, we have been muzzled, we have been crushed, we have been abused, we have been left out, but we are here because we believe. We believe in God the Father, God the Son, God the Holy Spirit, and we support our male congregants." But they are in a place to which they come and have been sitting quietly, waiting for God to speak to their situation. They have been waiting for God to speak to their hurt. They have been waiting for God to remove the stigma of what they have experienced and regarded to be disgraceful because of their foul experiences. They have had to be quiet because Uncle So-and-So was messing with them, because Deacon Such-and-Such is home beating up his wife, and because the church knows that that father has been touching his child and did not have any

---

[56] Assualt, South Eastern Center Against Sexual. *South Eastern CASA*. March 13, 2017. https://www.secasa. com.au/pages/feelings-after-sexual-assault/ (accessed 06 06, 2018).

business touching her "there." The church knows that the husband is raping his wife. Many feel that, since the couple is married, she does not have the right to say "no," and that the man has the right to take "it." Not so! The church has come to the place where the time is now.

The hurts of women reach far past the need for a breakthrough, praying for a spouse, financial blessing, and basic, everyday needs. This sermon emphasized that leaders and laity are missing the heart of the matter. The heart of the matter is the fact that women are hurting differently, and women are the majority of the makeup of our churches. The church takes their tithes, offerings, and time through the responsibilities delegated to them. But, yet, the church is silent to their pain, or the women are told to just get over it. It is said to women, "You better not say nothing, and you better not embarrass this family." Or it is said, "Don't bring that foolishness in this church." Or they say, "Hussy, you shouldn't have been so fresh." Or worse, they say, "If your skirts were long enough, you wouldn't entice the men to look at you." But, yet, as women, they cry, "I've been hurt, and I've been violated, and I'm coming to my church because that is what I believe in, and that's all I know."

As one who has experienced and witnessed sexual and physical abuse, the portion of Scripture that was most profound, enlightening, and encouraging was "to bind up the broken-hearted." Rachel St. Clair, a womanist theologian, made it a point in her article to explain the binding from the perspective of Black women.[57] She implies that we, as Black women, see God not from the perspective that we are tied to Jesus in His struggles, in Jesus's hurts, pains, and suffering, but that Jesus is tied together with us in our suffering, struggle, strife, hurt, and disappointment. Jesus is not holding onto us in order for us to carry His cross. Jesus is

---

[57] St. Clair, Raquel. "Womanist Biblical Interpretation." *True to Our Native Land: An African American New Testament Commentary*, 2007: 54–62.

sustaining us during our cross-bearing events. In essence, Jesus has already borne His cross, and in the binding of Jesus to us, solidifies Jesus's promise to never leave us or forsake us.

This prophetic sermon concluded with sounding the trumpet and giving the prophetic clarion call to churches, leaders, and congregations to break the silence of sexual and physical abuses against women globally, that this is the acceptable year of the Lord, and the time is now for the church to step forward to join in the fight to dismantle the plague of sexual and physical abuse against women.

After each sermon, the congregation (laity and leaders) completed a weekly congregation survey with ten questions. The sample population for this set of surveys is twenty-five, which does not include the fifteen who participated and submitted a similar weekly form for the focus discussion group; therefore, making the intended sample size to forty. However, there were a few who committed to participate but later stated there would possibly be a week or two they would not be able to attend for personal reasons. These persons indicated their desire or need to participate; therefore, the worship services were recorded weekly, and a video link was emailed or texted to the participants who were absent. For the first week, there was a 68 percent survey participation rate.

- Sermon topic was clearly expressed: 94 percent
- The sermon challenged their level of comfort in a manner that is impactful and life-altering with respect to the issue: 94 percent
- The sermon enhanced or enlightened their understanding of the scripture text: 76 percent
- Based on the sermon, did it encourage to reengage the text through a different lens: 64 percent
- Was the sermon relevant to the issues concerning the victimization of women today: 94 percent

- Was the sermon relative to the issue of sexual and physical abuse: 88 percent
- The sermon frustrated, angered, or disturbed them: 47 percent agree; 17 percent somewhat agree; 23 percent do not agree.
- The sermon promoted self-reflection: 64 percent agreed; 23 percent disagreed.
- Are likely to share or reference this sermon with others: 76 percent
- The sermon is helpful in promoting personal awareness of sexual and physical abuses of women and the need to break the silence: 70 percent

The majority of the congregation expressed that the sermon, "The Time Is Now," was germane to the issues concerning victimization of women today. They also expressed that the sermon challenged their level of comfortability in a manner that was impactful and life-altering (increase in knowledge). The sermon also caused them to re-engage the sermonic text to view from a different lens. The majority also indicated the sermon disturbed them and caused self-reflection. Lastly, the sermon was helpful in promoting personal awareness of sexual and physical abuses of women and the need to break the silence.

The focus group reconvened downstairs in the lower sanctuary immediately following the worship experience. The focus group had a participation rate of 80 percent. The focus group yielded the same results. Seven of their questions are identical to the weekly congregation's survey questions. There was one question that required them to write in their response. Many shared the same response, but there were a few that were different. However, all of the responses were conclusions drawn from the preached word. Some of the responses were

- The sermon topic was clear: 100 percent
- The sermon was relative to the issue of sexual and physical abuse: 100 percent
- The sermon encouraged them: 100 percent
- The sermon either frustrated, angered, or disturbed them negatively: 50 percent reflects; 25 percent somewhat reflects; .08 percent does not reflect.[58]
- The sermon promoted self-reflection: 100 percent
- The sermon gave them a sense of empowerment over the experience of abuse (minimizing the shame associated with abuse): 100 percent
- They would share the sermon and related materials with others: 100 percent
- The combination of the sermon and weekly reflective-group discussion are effective: 83 percent
- The group discussions about the sermon was helpful in promoting personal healing: 100 percent
- (This question is qualitative as opposed to quantitative). The following information is what the eleven out of thirteen participants answered as to what they took away from this sermon:
  o The church and the pulpit need to address the hurt of women.
  o God is here for them.
  o It's time to speak up and out, not just those victimized, but also the church as a whole. The church's silence is no longer acceptable.
  o It's time to take a stand against domestic violence.
  o Women are important in the church.

---

[58] This question was asked because of the possible intensity of the discussions to help identify anyone that may have a higher level of distress, and, if necessary, ensure they were connected to a clinician immediately.

o The church is coming to a new level.
o The statistics were very alarming.
o Laws reinforce a male perspective.
o There is too much sexual abuse in our community.
o The matter is real, and it's not being addressed.
o Systemic society is male-dominated and particularly of European/Caucasian views.

The concerns of the group are valid and informed. Each participant strongly affirmed the positive impact of the discussion of the preached word and the ability to be able to reflect, ask questions, and interject into the discussion. They valued the ability to share their opinion and were comfortable in sharing their experiences and their personal feelings. Some expressed their frustration of no one affirming them, letting them know that it was not their fault. They expressed their frustration of how, in the church, the girl or woman is made to feel ashamed and the boy or man is never made to be accountable. They referenced the young pregnant teenage girl being brought before the church to apologize for getting pregnant, but the boy is never made to come forward. They discussed how sex is something taboo in the church and how the church steers away from any mention of sex, even with married couples. Anything about sexuality is taboo. These concerns connect to the church's inability and unwillingness to talk about sexual violations and standing up for those who have been violated. Because sex is such a taboo subject, rapes, molestations, incest, and other violations are hushed. Some even spoke about how some sexual violations were disguised as love—love and attention from an older man was flattering; however, never realizing that it was statutory rape, the rape of an innocent person.

There was an issue of sexism that also erupted in the group discussion. Someone brought up having a problem with women being deacons and that it was a male role in the church. The issue was addressed tactfully with the Scripture, pointing out that God's Spirit is poured out on all flesh, and both men and women shall prophesy. It was also pointed out that Deborah was a woman judge in the Old Testament, and that Scripture is misinterpreted when taken out of its historical context. This was a very important topic to discuss. It speaks to how the male voice had dictated to women for so long, especially the dominant patriarchal voice of the Scriptures that have been preached and reproached from different people, both male and female. As preachers, this is one of the systemic evils that we must overcome to be effective in dismantling the silence in the church regarding brutal violations and perversions against women.

There were some positive suggestions to help facilitate the church moving forward against sexual and domestic violence. It was suggested that the congregation might start with a mentorship and etiquette ministry for young women to help increase their self-esteem, self-image, and self-worth so that they respect themselves and know their value so that others will respect them also. The first night was a great beginning for the overall project. One of the participants thanked me, on paper and aloud, for the process and for being the first to bring it into the church and for the church being called to a new level; everyone agreed. However, I expressed that this is just the beginning, and we have a journey ahead of us. The congregation looked forward to the following worship experiences, sermons, and discussions.

Sermon Two

The second sermon, "Can't You Hear Her?" from Judges 19:22–26, was preached using the hermeneutical and homiletical style of incarnational translation. This sermon was creative, effective, transformative, and challenging. The sermon challenged and disturbed the comfort of the participants and the preacher. Using the incarnational translation approach, it was necessary to explain the technique in order for the congregation to know that the Scripture was not being distorted or taken out of context. The explanation included modernizing the text as well as sharing the story as a dramatic expression (incarnate, Word becoming flesh). Prior to explaining the technique, it was necessary to read the text in its entirety. However, the text was divided into three portions and read at different intervals during the worship experience. Because of the uniqueness of the technique, it was imperative for the congregation to be familiar with the pericope. Not wanting to assume that everyone was familiar with the rape of Tamar, 2 Samuel 13 was read by three different persons. Permitting congregants to participate in the order of service allowed them to own the moment and be open to the experience.

The dramatization also required someone to participate in the role of Ammon, who was renamed Anthony. Thoughtful consideration was given to who would play the part of Ammon. Initially, the pastor of the church was considered; however, the thought of the congregation seeing him in the role of an abuser was not appropriate, even if it was not real. The same thought went forward concerning any of the other leaders of the church. Another concern was the recent and seemingly continuous incidents concerning ecumenical leaders sexually abusing women and children, some of them family members. Also, a close male friend of mine was briefly considered but was also dismissed because I did not want others to think I may be currently involved in an abusive relationship. Finally, one of the brothers of the church who participates in various skits within the church was asked to assist in this performance, and he agreed. The brother who agreed to participate received the skit prior to doing the skit but not before he volunteered to help.

He informed the preacher that the skit angered him and could not have imagined this being in the Scriptures and was unfamiliar with the biblical story. The skit was physical, confrontational, and written to be very realistic. He also revealed later that night that he found it difficult to explain to his wife the role he was playing; however, after the skit, he took the manuscript home to share with his wife, as well as sharing the sermonic message.

Incarnational translation and transformational preaching have commonness. Both include the importance of the preacher embodying the sermon, the ability to intentionally draw the hearer into and experience the sermon, and bringing awareness to a particular issue, attitude, or characteristic. Also, it impacts change in action, deed, or behavior in an outward, inward, or both as an intentional response to the preached word. The translation and the enactment were written to cause the hearer to enter into a dimension that would closely reflect the experience of not only Tamar but also many who have experienced intimate abuse. The purpose was also to increase one's knowledge by making one aware of the issues underlying rape and the negative impact of silence.

The sermon began with offering a perspective or voice that was different from how one may have experienced or read it prior to that night. It introduced the voice and retelling of the story by the niece of Tamar, Absalom's daughter. The niece's understanding and retelling of the story came from stories that were handed down to her or overheard from women in the community that gossiped and speculated about the rape of Tamar and her absconding. However, it never seemed that any of these ladies were trying to speak up on her behalf, still leaving her silenced and left to live in shame. This is too much like many women who have been hurt and sit silently amongst the congregation without being acknowledged, supported, encouraged, affirmed, and offered the opportunity to tell their story and reclaim their voices. In all of this, the church, congregation, and the women in the community are still silent, as though they could not hear her quieted and hushed pain. In this sermonic depiction, we explored the rape of Tamar by allowing Tamar to take us on a modern-day journey of her account of her rape by her half-brother, her voice, and what she experienced.

The sermon continued and addressed the various forms of incestuous rape. Rape from a brother, half-brother, father, uncle, or cousin who manipulated the trust and love of innocent women and girls, instilling fear and causing silence, embarrassment, and displaced shame. Rape is a catastrophic invasion of women that does not have boundaries. Rape affects women of all ages, races, ethnicities, cultures, and worlds. Because of this fact, the preacher identified names of women who can be associated with a national origin, not as racial profiling, but for the purposes of making and validating a point, names, such as Marcia (Mar-see-ah), Svetlana, Isabella, Beth, and Tamar. Throughout the sermon, Tamar purposefully maintains her name so as not to lose the congregation's focus and connection to the Scripture and the woman. Tamar led us from the point of her having to go and prepare food for "Anthony," to an account of his rape against her, then having been thrown out, her shame, her telling her brother "Odell," him calming, hushing, and silencing her, and even her father's lack of response to her hurt and how he had quickly looked to the welfare of his son, the rapist. Just as Tamar's father, the congregation still continues to dismiss the hurt of women as though they do not hear their tears and do not desire to hear their stories, as the women continue to be ostracized, subjected to ridicule, ignored, and silenced.

My question is, "Do you hear her? Do you hear them? Are you going to break the silence," not just the silence of the church, but also the silenced voices of the victimized? The *time is now* to hear them, the victimized, to also love them, encourage them, listen to them, and free their voices from the vault of the places they had been violated, and to empower them to tell their stories in their own voices."

Fifty-two percent of the participants filled out and submitted the weekly congregation survey questionnaire for this sermon, "Can't You Hear Her?" Of that percentage, the survey yielded the following results:

- Sermon topic was clearly expressed: 69 percent
- The sermon challenged their level of comfortability in a manner that is impactful and life-altering in respect to the issue: 69 percent
- The sermon enhanced or enlightened their understanding of the scripture text: 69 percent
- Based on the sermon, did it encourage to re-engage the text through a different lens: 92 percent
- Was the sermon relevant to the issues concerning the victimization of women today: 92 percent
- Was the sermon relative to the issue of sexual and physical abuse: 92 percent
- The sermon frustrated, angered, or disturbed them: 92 percent
- The sermon promoted self-reflection: 69 percent
- Are likely to share or reference this sermon with others: 92 percent
- The sermon is helpful in promoting personal awareness of sexual and physical abuses of women and the need to break the silence: 92 percent

This sermon has been determined to be transformative and very effective in its delivery and relativity. The sermon increased the congregant's awareness of rape as well as their understanding of the need for the church to break the silence. It appears the congregation was either disturbed, angered, or frustrated enough about the issue to have the desire to approach the subject matter and respond positively by sharing the information gained with others. Having been approached by the congregants, many shared they had never heard of the text or have never heard of the rape of Tamar. They also expressed that the skit was shocking, they enjoyed the realness of the skit, and it gave them a different perspective about sexual abuse.

The sermon incited much discussion in the focus group as well as personal disclosure. There was an 86 percent attendance and participation rate of the focus group and their responses to the weekly focus group survey questions. The results of the survey questions were as follows:

- The sermon topic was clear: 100 percent
- The sermon was relative to the issue of sexual and physical abuse: 100 percent
- The sermon encouraged them: 100 percent
- The sermon either frustrated, angered, or disturbed them negatively: 46 percent agreed; 46 percent disagreed; .07 percent no response. [59]
- The sermon promoted self-reflection: 76 percent
- The sermon gave them a sense of empowerment over the experience of abuse (minimizing the shame associated with abuse): 76 percent, and 15 percent no response.
- They would share the sermon and related materials with others: 100 percent
- The combination of the sermon and weekly reflective-group discussion are effective: 100 percent

---

[59] This question was asked because of the possible intensity of the discussions to help identify anyone that may have a higher level of distress, and, if necessary, ensure they are connected to a clinician immediately.

- The group discussions about the sermon was helpful in promoting personal healing: 100 percent
- (This question is qualitative as opposed to quantitative). The following information is what the eleven out of thirteen participants answered as to what they took away from this sermon:
  o It was not my fault.
  o It is not your fault when some girls (boys) are molested. Seek help; tell someone.
  o It's not my fault.
  o God loves me, and it's not my fault.
  o Acts of violence, such as this, affects not just the person but the many people surrounding the person.
  o Abuse of women has always existed.
  o Woman are sexually abused but stay quiet about it, but it's time to speak up.
  o The difference between how rape is viewed by gender, male/female.
  o This abuse happens a lot.
  o How society ignores the cries of abused women!
  o Very relevant to the times, unfortunately!

This session was intense and informative. There were some who shared how they had experienced or have knowledge of sexual and physical violence. The Tamar dramatization was impactful and discomforting for this group. One of the discussions shared how the skit allowed them to see into the life incident of those who experience sexual and domestic abuse. It was discussed that having to respond to those in the medical field as a result of the abuse was much different than she had imagined. The skit gave insight into how and what battered and raped women went through, the struggle to survive an attack, the struggle to maintain until one is able to reach out for help, and the helplessness of victims at the hand of their abuser. The skit shocked them, and they were not prepared for that visual experience. On the contrary, many discussed the ingenuity of presenting the pericope in the manner of a skit. These points and observations provoked great discussion and reflection.

Another discussion that was therapeutic was the factor of running away from the experience of sexual abuse to only run into the comfort of substance abuse. The experience of the sermon became very real and self-reflective to some individuals. They discussed how they wanted to get up and run. They remembered the account of their experience, but they could not run. There was nowhere to go but to confront their fear. They could not run to drugs; the only place to run to was God. This testimony took the discussion in a direction that was not expected, and it was not rejected. Truthfully, I was fearful of what was coming next, but I was comforted with knowing there were clinicians in place should they be needed. However, they spoke about how this experience was the beginning of healing. They were grateful for the revelation, the affirmation of those in the group, and the ability to face fears and know that God is here. There were others who shared as well and were thankful for this research preaching series, the discussion sessions, and the comradery of the group.

Issues of shame and lying to cover up the truth of what was happening, and the silence and insensitivity of even family members and friends were discussed. The discussions in the focus group were not only about getting the word out and breaking the silence in the church, but also, it became the beginning of the healing process for many. Healing is necessary to embrace others who are silently suffering and help them to move past suppressing memories so they may begin healing too. During this time, the importance of seeking counseling without the fear of being ashamed was expressed.

Also discussed was the inability of some pastors to offer effective counseling for those who have experienced sexual and domestic abuse. In addition to negative aggressive responses to women who reveal these issues, some shared that, instead of pastors saying they are not equipped to help and refer out to professionals, they do more harm to the victim, especially when they seemingly take the side of the abuser with victim and abuser in the same session together. Weighing in is the influence and threats by family members of victims to remain silent and not say a word, along with families knowing the abuse is going on but not saying anything. They equated it to Tamar's story of how it seemingly had a detrimental effect on her over the years of being held captive by silence. They all noted that it was most important to speak up and speak out. Lastly, all agreed that this is a much-needed preaching series, and abuse can no longer be swept under the rug. It is time to break the silence and it is time to "hear her."

Sermon Three

Sermon three, "The Absence of the Presence of God," Judges 19:22–26, began with two important scriptures that seemingly parenthetically encapsulated the pericope of the unnamed concubine. Chapter 19:1 begins with this phrase that seemingly establishes the mindset and hearts of the people of God throughout the land, "In those days there was no king in Israel," and chapter 21:25, the end of Judges and the finality of the unnamed concubine's injustice, concludes with, "In those days there was no king in Israel: all the people did what was right in their own eyes." These two portions of scriptures led this sermon in the direction of exposing the root of this horrible story. When there was no king in the land, there was no leadership or moral compass to lead, direct, or rebuke the actions of the people. The moral compass of the people was broken, and their hearts strayed from and did not seek God's presence. Bill Wiese, in his book, *23 Minutes in Hell: One Man's Story about What He Saw, Heard, and Felt in that Place of Torment*, speaks of the darkness, eeriness, stench, and feeling of hopelessness. He mentions that the worse thing about being in hell was the feeling of the "absence of the presence of God. "[60] The darkness in the hearts of the people led them to believe and do what they perceived was okay, not based on the law of God nor the law of the land. Because of the lack of the presence of God, not only in the land, but particularly in the hearts of the people, this absence of the presence of God led to the horrifying gang rape of the unnamed concubine.

This sermon addressed several systemic issues that were contributable to the unjustifiable gang rape of the unnamed concubine and the life of a battered woman who is thrown to wolves, so to speak, at the hand of her "husband," the Levite, a man of God. The unnamed concubine's story begins at the onset of chapter 19. She had absconded from the Levite who came seeking her at her father's house to return home with him. The story speaks to the father convincing the Levite to stay for a few days, which led to their delay of returning home. In this story, the mother is not spoken of, seen, or heard of the entire time the unnamed concubine is home. There is no dialogue between the mother and daughter about her dilemma; however, the father is intentional in delaying their departure. This makes one wonder why a father would return his daughter to an abusive relationship and why he held them back from leaving. Perhaps he was trying to calm the Levite down. He was most likely very angry that he had to travel a day's distance to retrieve his "wife," his concubine. Perhaps the father was very

---

[60] Wiese, Bill. 23 Minutes In Hell: One Man's Story About What He Saw, Heard, and Felt in that Place of Torment. Lake Mary: Charisma House, 2006.

familiar with the cycle of violence. For the unnamed concubine, being exposed to and growing up in a home with domestic violence is part of a generational curse. Was the father beating his wife also? We never hear anything from her, particularly any opposition of her daughter leaving with this man. Women have been fearful of speaking out against sexual and domestic violence for years, even when it affects and is a violation against their own children. Fear is crippling. If you have never experienced the level of fear that makes one freeze in response to threats, to be silent even when they want to speak out, a fear that causes one to make decisions in the moment without thinking because you cannot think, just react in a manner that is believable as to receive the least amount of bodily harm. Fear is an emotional stronghold that needs to be broken from the lives, spirits, and hearts of those who have been and still are being victimized. This sermon spoke to the power of fear as well as the power of the love of God needed to overcome the beaten-in fear of victims.

The actions or lack of action taken by the father took away the choice of the unnamed concubine. Not only was her voice taken away but also the voices of the virgin daughters were taken as well. Their father, also, voluntarily offered them out to the savages who came to rape the Levite. For too long, men have taken the position of speaking on behalf of women, to tell them what to do, to acquire women like property, and treat women less than human. Men make major decisions on what women should be allowed to do with their own bodies, careers, and education in an effort to limit the ability and success of women. These men, the father of the virgin daughters and the Levite, appeared to be men of God. However, they did not operate as men of God or protectors of God's people, particular the daughters and women of God. Even today, we see women having to protect the integrity of the family as opposed to men protecting the family through self-sacrifice.

Women have had to be self-sacrificing for the sake of the family. These women were offered up for the protection of the Levite and the sake of the hospitable man, to save face in the eyes of those formidable men. These men violated the trust these women had in them as fathers, lovers, protectors, and men of God, just as the men who have been exposed as pedophiles and rapists.

Recently, approximately 188 names of Catholic priests and deacons accused of sexual abuse of minors dating as far back as 1940, all men supposedly men of God, were released. [61] They violated the trust of many while operating in the role of God's servant leaders. Also, the Pope acknowledged knowing that for years, nuns have been raped and impregnated by priests and have had abortions as a result of becoming impregnated from the rape. [62] The Southern Baptist Convention is also contending with 250 reprobate leaders who are accused of sexually abusing more than 700 congregants over the last twenty years.[63] An even more grotesque violation is the Brooklyn pastor accused of raping his own daughter repeatedly for multiple years.[64]

All of these individuals are men who were entrusted with souls of many, who were held in high esteem throughout various faith-based denominations, congregations, and demographical locations, yet their hearts, like those men in the Judges pericope, are

---

[61] Heyboer, Kelly and Ted Sherman. "NJ.com True Jersey." *nj.com*. February 13, 2019. http://www.nj.com (accessed February 26, 2019).

[62] Hopkins, Anna. "Fox News." *foxnews.com*. January 13, 2019. http://www.foxnews.com (accessed February 26, 2019).

[63] Phillips, Kristine and Amy B. Wang. "The Washington Post." February 10, 2019. https://www.washingtonpost.com/religion/2019/02/10/pure-evil-southern-baptist-leaders-condemn-decades-sexual-abuse-revealed-investigation/ (accessed February 17, 2019).

[64] Hopkins, Anna. "Fox News." foxnews.com. January 13, 2019. http://www.foxnews.com (accessed February 26, 2019).

suffering from a serious void, the absence of the presence of God. Instead, they have chosen to live in darkness and create a world of darkness in others through the use of fear. Victims are terrified to come forward, tell, and speak against the wishes of their fathers, husbands, protectors, and supposedly guardians of their souls and spiritual growth. At the base of these dark evils is the systemic root of patriarchy as well.

Dr. Traci C. West defines patriarchy as a "systemic devaluation of the worth and value of women."[65] In other words, patriarchy creates a gender imbalance or supremacy. This imbalance promotes and elevates the importance of men over women while devaluing the humanity of women by lowering women to the place of property, having the ability to do with or treat their "property" as they so desire. Unfortunately, we still live in such a degrading patriarchal society, and in many societies, worldwide, women are still equated as property and less than, and are under the subjection of brutality and sexual and physical assault, including genital mutilations simply because they are women. Unfortunately, the political arena is still allowing the fear and silencing of victims to continue by publicly discrediting women who have courageously stepped forward against men of power and men who are aspiring to attain positions of power in *this* country. These men in our patriarchal society exercise their White privilege, political status, and affiliations to eradicate themselves from any accusations or forms of persecution while trying to destroy the women who finally have gained the courage to step forward and break the silence.

Throughout the harsh violations in this pericope and in society today, this sermon still offered hope to the congregation. Although the hearts and consciences of evil-controlled and indulged men whose hearts are dark because of the absence of God in their lives,

---

[65] West, Traci C. Wounds of the Spirit: Black Women, Violence, and Resistance Ethics. New York and London: New York University Press, 1999.

God is not absent in ours. God never appears to step in this story of the unnamed concubine, yet God is there. God has given humankind free will. That free will allows humankind to decide to have a heart after God or have a dark heart of evil, a heart lacking God's presence. Because it is true to the character of God, God does not violate the will of the men in this story, as well as the men in the world that purposely commit heinous acts of physical and sexual offenses against women. Nevertheless, those violators will be held accountable to God. We do not hear of God in this pericope or the dark places of the unnamed concubine's experience. She probably wondered, "God, where are you?"

The sermon continued to remind everyone that in the dark places in our lives, the ugly experiences of our lives, our God is always present. Even in the presence of evil, God will sustain us through dark and harsh times. They were further encouraged to not give up on God. God has each of us even when going through difficulties and the harshness of life. So, have confidence and have faith. The Word of God says, "Vengeance is Mine, I will repay, says the Lord. "[66] God has not and did not punish those victimized. In situations like this, it is very difficult to see, feel, hear, and even believe in God, but belief and trust in God's promise to never leave or disown us is crucial. Be encouraged. Even in the absence of the presence of God in the hearts of abusers, God is always present.

64 percent of the participants filled out and submitted the weekly congregation survey questionnaires for this sermon, "The Absence of the Presence of God. " Of that percentage, the survey yielded the following results:

- Sermon topic was clearly expressed: 81 percent

[66] Deuteronomy 32:35 (New King James Version).

- The sermon challenged their level of comfortability in a manner that is impactful and life-altering in respect to the issue: 87. 5 percent
- The sermon enhanced or enlightened their understanding of the scripture text: 100 percent
- Based on the sermon, did it encourage to re-engage the text through a different lens: 75 percent
- Was the sermon relevant to the issues concerning the victimization of women today: 100 percent
- Was the sermon relative to the issue of sexual and physical abuse: 100 percent
- The sermon frustrated, angered, or disturbed them: 100 percent
- The sermon promoted self-reflection: 81 percent
- Are likely to share or reference this sermon with others: 100 percent
- The sermon is helpful in promoting personal awareness of sexual and physical abuses of women and the need to break the silence: 100 percent

The congregation's survey responses to this sermon reflected that the majority understood the sermon topic and the information transmitted. The majority also revealed that they believed the sermon was impactful and life-altering in their understanding of the pericope and the issues that contribute to the act of rape, fear, and silence. The sermon was responsive to the issue of physical and sexual abuse, increased their knowledge of the subject, and helped them to understand this scripture better. It caused them to want to re-engage the text and read the full story and promote their personal awareness regarding the need to break the silence about these violations against women, inspiring them to share the information and sermon with others. There were some in the congregation that verbally expressed they were not familiar with this story, that they had never read it and never heard of it before that night. Quite naturally, they said they had never heard it preached before that night as well. Additionally, many said they were grateful for the incorporating of current events to making the sermon relevant for today. Today, we are in perilous times that are disheartening and seemingly negatively infectious to the world.

The focus group reconvened downstairs in the lower sanctuary immediately following the worship experience. There was an 86 percent participation rate of those in the focus group, and the results of their survey are as follows:

- The sermon topic was clear: 100 percent
- The sermon was relative to the issue of sexual and physical abuse: 100 percent
- The sermon encouraged them: 100 percent
- The sermon either frustrated, angered of disturbed them negatively: 53 percent agreed; 15 percent disagreed. [67]
- The sermon promoted self-reflection: 76 percent agree; 15 percent no reply
- The sermon gave them a sense of empowerment over the experience of abuse (minimizing the shame associated with abuse): 84 percent agree; .07 percent disagree; and .07 percent no response
- They would share the sermon and related materials with others: 76 percent
- The combination of the sermon and weekly reflective-group discussion are effective: 92 percent

---

[67] This question was asked because of the possible intensity of the discussions to help identify anyone that may have a higher level of distress, and, if necessary, ensure they are connected to a clinician immediately.

- The group discussions about the sermon was helpful in promoting personal healing: 100 percent
- (This question is qualitative as opposed to quantitative). The following information is what the eleven out of thirteen participants answered as to what they took away from this sermon:
  o Systemic evil; the women in the Bible had no justice, but now they have a voice through us women of the church.
  o Women have been abused forever.
  o There is nothing new happening today.
  o Women had no power.
  o No matter what you're going though in this "man's world," God knows, heals, and will take care of you!
  o Sadly, some things have not changed.
  o Women have historically been treated as property and sacrifices. Even though these horrific things happen, God is with us, and He loves us.

This group discussion began with me sharing my struggle with writing this sermon and feeling as though the unnamed concubine had been betrayed by the sermon. I expressed that I did not feel as though her voice was heard and that her gang rape was dismissed because I spoke more of the systemic evil. However, it became apparent that her rape extended beyond her physical violation to the root of the evil that speaks to the life-long violations of women throughout history. My heart went out to the unnamed concubine. I believe it went out to her because she is unnamed, and perhaps she remained nameless because she represents so many women at the same time then and now. She was gang raped, raped by the variations of evil, each in the form of those men.

The group responded to the plight and stated the sermon was very effective and powerful. The sermon told her story and the unnamed concubine spoke volumes without saying a word. They stated they were able to identify with her pain, her family history, the abusive relationship she was in, her rape, and her faithfulness to get back to the house for shelter, only to be betrayed. The group commented on the tone of the preacher's voice, which gave them a calm assurance although the acts were violent. The voice instilled humility into the hearer, allowing them to feel what the women were feeling and experiencing as though they were there, which moved them to a place of compassion.

One of the women in the group shared a story of a woman in Australia who was a Black Panther named Marlene Cummings, and how she was in a documentary for Black History Month sharing her experience of the abuse of men and their feeling that they have the right to abuse women. She stated that the story of the concubine being gang raped all night reminded her of this woman because she had also shared that she had been raped all night as well. The woman had gone to an international Black Panther event, and two guys had invited her to go to a party with them only to find out she was the party and they had raped her all night. She survived, but it was truly a disheartening violation because it was someone she knew and trusted like an "uncle," as she had affection-ately called him. She continued to say that women were silent and never shared all the abuse that was happening in the organization because they were more concerned about the movement.

Another person brought up the question of how a father can be willing to have his own daughter violated for the sake of someone else, particularly for a man. This was puzzling to the group of how a man would do this. They were reminded that everyone has a choice to choose either good or evil, and sometimes we do not choose the good. However, there is a difference between being overcome with an evil decision and occasions when your life is just darkness. There is no God in them. They continued the conversation and spoke about the evil demonic forces that actually overtake the lives of individuals and generational curses as the cause of behaviors. Abusers may have witnessed abuse all their lives and grew into being an abuser because that is how they know to behave. Or, as someone mentioned, the generational curse that concerned them was the possibility of them having children, little girls who would also become victims of sexual abuse. Another form of generational curse that was discussed was the possibility of the children in abusive homes growing up and being attracted to men who are abusive because that is all they know. One of the participants also talked about the "sickness" of abuse and mental disorders. Not everyone agreed, but they did take it all into consideration.

One person in the group called our attention back to the strangers coming to the house, specifically looking for *him*, the Levite. She mentioned the shocking revelation that they came for *a man* and not a woman, which led them to understand and comment that the same thing is going on now as then. They were raping men as well as women in the Scriptures, just as they are raping boys and men now. This information was very shocking to them but worth mentioning.

This night, the group really dissected the story, recalled, and commented on every portion, even speaking to the lack of presence of the mother/wife and that there was no mention. They recalled how women today are silent as well. Sometimes women are living in fear and, therefore, they are quiet about situations because of fear that is crippling and immobilizing. They shared a story about how a father raped all of his daughters and how, once the oldest was a senior in high school, she finally had the courage to expose what was going on in her house, and the mother was seemingly silent. We made it a point not to be judgmental of others because one never knows the underlying story. Even when sharing historical events, it is imperative not to judge because judging is what still holds those in the pew hostage to silence and the fear of being shamed. Another fear is the fear of consequences. Not that they are fearful of what would happen to them but what would happen if they reported to their father the rape or abuse. They feared their father would retaliate and go to jail. This fear is identified as losing a parent to rage of retaliation.

The group also mentioned the sermon title was very effective. "The Absence of the Presence of God," reminded them that God had not left them during the time of their own abusive situation. The focus group had, by this time, developed into a community, a loving, encouraging, and embracing community. In this community, they helped one of their own to celebrate six days of sobriety and committed to love and assist her in the journey daily.

Sermon Four

"What's Love Got to Do with It?" was the fourth and final sermon of this series. The sermonic text was Genesis 34, the narrative of the ravishment of Dinah. The reading of this text was incorporated into the order of service because of its length and the importance of familiarizing the audience with her entire story. It was divided into three segments, read by three attendees. This is another scandalous portion of Scripture that recounts the heinous defilement of a woman, a portion that many had not read or heard prior to the night that this was preached. The preaching of this sermon uncovered multiple variations of manipulation, coercion, and sexism that accompanied the rape of Dinah. Unfortunately, these infractions upon Dinah are imposed upon her by those who claim to love her and are supposed to love her. Her rapist commits the first offense in the name of *"love. "*

The account of Dinah is an anomalous and distorted narrative of a love story. Dinah's rapist ravaged her and then fell in love with her as a result of his lustful abomination. The question is asked, "What's love got to do with it?" This title is derived from the movie about the abuse of Tina Turner at the hands of her husband, Ike Turner. In the instance of Dinah's rape, like Tina's beatings, love had nothing to do with it. This was just another example of sexism, privilege, and political status diminishing the voice, choice, and rights of a woman. Shechem, the privileged rapist, not only forces himself on her sexually, but also engages his father to acquire her as his wife. Shechem demands his father approach and plead with Dinah's father, Jacob, after he has forcefully deflowered her, so he might be betrothed to Dinah. This betrothal is another violation against Dinah, against her voice, against her well-being, and perhaps it may be psychologically damaging as well. During the betrothed period, Dinah would be forced to live under the same roof as her abuser. Sadly, there are many women who have had this cruel psychological and emotional experience. Women have had to grow up in houses with their abusers without being allowed to express their fear or let anyone know what was happening to them because of debilitating fear. Women have been raped by their fathers, uncles, brothers, and cousins, and have been threatened into secrecy.

The parishioners needed to understand the power of fear, especially if they have never experienced fear in its fullness; therefore, fear was defined:

> Fear is a feeling induced by perceived danger or threat that occurs in certain types of organisms, which causes a change in metabolic and organ functions and ultimately a change in behavior, such as fleeing, hiding, or freezing from perceived traumatic events. Fear in human beings may occur in

response to a certain stimulus occurring in the present, or in anticipation or expectation of a future threat perceived as a risk to body or life. The fear response arises from the perception of danger leading to confrontation with or escape from/avoiding the threat, which in extreme cases of fear can be a freeze response or paralysis.[68]

The importance of the definition of fear to be read was to stop any judgments toward victims and avoid hurtful questions, such as, "Why didn't you leave?" or statements saying, "I would've left," never having had the experience. The dismantling of judgment is important to encourage people not to judge abusive situations from the outside in, causing the injured to be reinjured.

The second man in Dinah's circle to give her a distorted love is her father, Jacob. Shechem and his father, Hamor, approach Jacob to ask for his daughter's hand in marriage after he had raped her. Jacob was furious about the rape, yet he entertained their proposal. Shechem and his father acknowledge the rape of Dinah to her father, but none of these men ever acknowledge Dinah, her feelings, or her thoughts. Instead, they try to keep peace between two nations at the expense of the sacrifice of Dinah's wholeness.

Regrettably, this is only the first recorded time of Jacob's betrayal of Dinah. Further down in this pericope, Jacob puts his interest first for the sake of his name and nation. Again, at the expense of Dinah, Jacob is more concerned about his image. Too often in our society and in cultures today, we find mothers and fathers silencing their daughters about sexual abuse by a relative for the sake of the family name. Children, daughters, and women should not be responsible for upholding the family name at the cost of sacrificing their own lives, purity, and sanity.

---

[68] Bing.com.

The last persons preached in this event that violated Dinah are her brothers. Interestingly, although they did violate Dinah, I admire their reasoning and efforts to protect the integrity of their sister. They devised and instituted a very evil and vile plan that worked. There were several issues with this plan: first, they perverted the sacredness of the covenant of circumcision that was established between Israel and God. Second, they never inquired of Dinah how she felt or what she wanted to do; they, too, dismissed her voice. And lastly, they destroyed all the men in Hamor's region, including Hamor and Shechem, leaving the women of that region unprotected and left to survive on their own. They did not take into consideration the adverse effect they would have on a multitude of other women. They wanted to avenge the dishonoring of Dinah's rape while terrorizing and devastating a plethora of other women. The biblical, patriarchal, and sexist behavior imposed on behalf of women are detrimental to women, not a help, just as it is in our society now.

Laws are made and passed today on behalf of women without allowing women to maintain their individual voices and choices. Am I Pro-Life? Yes, I am. Am I Pro-Choice? Yes, I am. I understand that choice belongs to the individual woman, and her voice should never be taken away. The dichotomy of Pro-Life or Pro-Choice affects so many decisions, rights, and privileges on a spectrum that is much greater than the right to have an abortion or the right to stop abortion. It is akin to the decision of the brothers of Dinah to manipulate the law of God (circumcision) to where the effect is beyond one person. The repercussions of those issues threaten the welfare of women, as well as women's rights to make informed decisions, be taken seriously as equals, and be seen as women in authority and leadership. I am sure the movement meant well, but I do not believe they understood the long-standing and adverse impact that it would have on the voice, credibility, equality, and integrity of all women.

Now that the distortion of love had been fleshed out, then I asked the question, "What does love got to do with it?" Love has everything to do with it, and it is not "a second-hand emotion." "Love is patient; love is kind; love is not envious or boastful or arrogant or rude. It does not insist on its own way; it is not irritable or resentful; it does not rejoice in wrongdoing but rejoices in the truth. It bears all things, believes all things, hopes all things, endures all things. Love never ends."[69] Love is not abusive. Love is not accusatory. Love is not judgmental. Love is affirming. Love extends to all. We, the church, are the extension of God, and we must show love in all that we do. Showing love includes standing up for those who cannot stand up for themselves, showing love to those who have never experienced the love of God, giving love to those who have experienced abuse disguised as love. Love is the difference. What's love got to do with it? Everything!

To conclude the sermon, I used lyrics from a song by Miranda Curtis, "we are under an open heaven, where His glory shall be revealed. "[70] We united the last sermon in the dissertation series to the initial sermonic title and text, "The Time Is Now," and Isaiah 61:1–3, by quoting, "The spirit of the Lord God is upon me, because the Lord has anointed me; he has sent me to bring good news to the oppressed, to bind up the brokenhearted, to proclaim liberty to the captives, and release to the prisoners; to proclaim the year of the Lord's favor, and the day of vengeance of our God; to comfort all who mourn; to provide for those who mourn in Zion—to give them a garland instead of ashes, the oil of gladness instead of mourning, the mantle of praise instead of a faint spirit."

---

[69] 1 Corinthians 13:4–8. NRSV.

[70] Curtis, Miranda. "Open Heaven." Open Heaven: The Miranda Experience Live. Columbia / Fair Trade Services, 2018.

That we, the women, the congregation, "shall stand be called oaks of righteousness, the planting of the Lord, to display his glory!" We declared that we are the people of God. We are the church of the living God, and we are commanded to stand up for those who cannot stand up for themselves! We are the church that needs to extend the love of God! We are the church that cannot be judgmental! We are the ones who need to embrace those who do not know what it means to be genuinely embraced! This *is* the acceptable year of the Lord! This is the year, 2019. The time is now for the church to stand. The time is now for the church to no longer be silent. We can no longer be idle. We can no longer turn a deaf ear (I turned my back to the congregation). We must embrace those who have been victimized. We must love them with godly love because love is not a second emotion; love is the gift that comes from God. "For God so love the world that he gave his only Son, so that everyone who believes in him may not perish but may have eternal life. "[71]

This entire worship service was very high-spirited. The congregants worshiped as the praise and worship team ministered through song. The song "Open Heaven" by Miranda Curtis really led us into a place of personal worship that opened our hearts to expect a blessing from the Lord. Each night, the service was wonderful, but this night, it was more than wonderful. The experience ushered in the Holy Spirit in such a way that the Spirit lingered the entire service. It appeared that the lyrics of being "under an open heaven where His glory shall be revealed where the sin, sick shall be healed. " Feeling the presence of the Lord gave everyone hope. This hope was meeting the needs of the people. Those who were engulfed in the experience of being sexually and physically violated have been released from the bondage, shame, and fear that had accompanied the violation for so long. The culmination of the

---

[71] John 3:16.

entire service offered hope and the reassurance that the church will respond to the call that the time is now, in 2019. The church will not only hear all the women who have been brutalized but will now break the silence, embrace, and affirm them. And the evidence of the presence of the Lord is here. God has spoken through the transformative preached word, and the people responded.

Fifty-six percent of the participants filled out and submitted the weekly congregation survey questionnaires for this sermon, "What's Love Got to Do with It?" Of that percentage, the survey yielded the following results:

- Sermon topic was clearly expressed: 100 percent
- The sermon challenged their level of comfortability in a manner that is impactful and life-altering in respect to the issue: 92 percent
- The sermon enhanced or enlightened their understanding of the scripture text: 85 percent
- Based on the sermon, did it encourage to re-engage the text through a different lens: 78 percent
- Was the sermon relevant to the issues concerning the victimization of women today: 100 percent
- Was the sermon relative to the issue of sexual and physical abuse: 100 percent
- The sermon frustrated, angered, or disturbed them: 57 percent were affected, .07 percent somewhat, and 28 percent were not affected either way.
- The sermon promoted self-reflection: 78 percent
- Are likely to share or reference this sermon with others: 78 percent
- The sermon is helpful in promoting personal awareness of sexual and physical abuses of women and the need to break the silence: 100 percent

The congregation's survey responses to this sermon reflected that everyone understood the sermon topic and the information transmitted. Additionally, each person believed the sermon was impactful and life-altering in their understanding of the pericope and the issues that contribute to the act of rape, fear, and silence. The sermon was reflective to the issue of physical and sexual abuse, increased their knowledge of the subject, and helped them to understand this scripture better. It caused them to want to re-engage the text and read the full story, and it promoted their personal awareness and the need to break the silence about these violations against women, and they will share the information and the sermon with others. The previously mentioned information averaged an 88 percent agreement of those who took the survey. Again, some in the congregation verbally expressed they were not familiar with this story, they had never read it, and never heard of it before that night. They also mentioned they had never heard it preached before that night. Additionally, many said they were grateful for this sermon series and the boldness of the research project.

The focus group reconvened downstairs in the lower sanctuary immediately following the worship experience. There was a 71 percent participation rate of those in the focus group, due to the absence of some participants, and the results of their survey are as follows:

- The sermon topic was clear: 100 percent
- The sermon was relative to the issue of sexual and physical abuse: 100 percent
- The sermon encouraged them: 90 percent

- The sermon either frustrated, angered, or disturbed them negatively: 80 percent .[72]
- The sermon promoted self-reflection: 70 percent
- The sermon gave them a sense of empowerment over the experience of abuse (minimizing the shame associated with abuse): 70 percent
- They would share the sermon and related materials with others: 80 percent
- The combination of the sermon and weekly reflective-group discussion are effective: 90 percent
- The group discussions about the sermon was helpful in promoting personal healing: 100 percent
- (This question is qualitative as opposed to quantitative). The following information is what the eleven out of thirteen participants answered as to what they took away from this sermon:
  o Love will help heal. Love isn't irritable or abusive. Love is patient and kind. The actions of Dinah's brothers further disrespected and violated women of an entire city.
  o Only in the end did they address Dinah's experience.
  o Love doesn't hurt.
  o The church needs to address and be supportive of abused women.
  o The church must not be blind or turn a deaf ear, must love and embrace. The church is the extension of God.
  o Dinah's welfare was not considered; it was only mentioned at the end.
  o Felt the spirit of Dinah in me.
  o This is therapeutic.

---

[72] This question was asked because of the possible intensity of the discussions to help identify anyone that may have a higher level of distress, and, if necessary, ensure they are connected to a clinician immediately.

o   What's love got to do with it? Everything. The church needs to love and embrace.

o   Unfortunately, it was now discovered that the men in the group believed they were not allowed to comment, and they thought it was a "woman thang." This issue was addressed immediately, and one of the men began to comment and participate in the discussion. The participants in the focus group expressed the need for *this* to not stop. They felt as though they were just getting started, and the group had begun to embrace and support one another. After this project was over, they expressed that it could not be the end—the researcher must establish a way to continue this group and increase the number of people to be able to come and participate. They stated this was too good to let go. Many women declared they would continue to be there for anyone who needed them. They would be there for them. They also said that we had created more than a community of support, we had created a family. Our *family* needs to reach out to more people to offer affirmation and encouragement.

The question was asked, "What do you think about Dinah?" They began to express how they viewed Dinah as a bystander in her own life, that she was not included in the decisions and watched as others made choices that affected her without asking her. Just as it seems, at times, women are bystanders in life as men decide what's best for them.

Someone commented that the behavior of the brothers was very natural. If someone does something to your family, then you are ready to do whatever is necessary, including possibly killing them. However, they never thought about the fact that others were hurt, particularly many women, as a result to the brothers' reaction. That was an interesting point that brought awareness, which led us to make sure we are careful when responding to offenses emotionally without thinking it through, including the consequences.

Another shared how this research project and the effectiveness of breaking the silence through the sermons and discussions have empowered her to go back to school for psychology and biblical studies. She continued to share that she is going to share her own story of sexual exploitation to encourage and help others. I expressed to her the importance of making sure she received counseling herself and deal with her own scars before moving on to help others. I shared my personal experience of having to be transparent about my foul misfortunes with my family. I also shared the importance of addressing and confronting any relatable issues prior to the beginning of this project to ensure I had begun advanced healing before trying to help others. If I had not, I would stand a greater chance of "bleeding" on the people while trying to encourage, bring awareness, and break the silence in the church; therefore, hurting instead of helping. She thanked me for doing this project, encouraging them and leading them all to a place of self-healing, drawing them closer to God, the increase in faith, the increase in knowledge, and a community that allowed them to know that they are not alone.

One of the men shared the mental conflict with which he was struggling. He shared it was difficult to understand how men feel as though it is okay for someone to sexually take a woman who is not interested in being with him. He continued to say that he struggled to understand how men could possibly justify these atrocious attacks. He also spoke of the difficulty of hitting a woman, a woman who he considers to be a part of him. How could men beat on a woman was a mystery to him. Loving his woman reflects loving himself, so any form of violation is self-violation. Men should just walk away. He continued to say that the message of the research project is to break the silence and bring awareness to these abuses against women, but the Bible gives so many accounts of these abuses. Seemingly that is what they thought then as the norm, so what is the church teaching now?

A different man introduced his thoughts on the current events of music artist, R. Kelly and how R. Kelly is trying to play the role of a victim because he is being condemned and accused of being a pedophile. He continued to give his opinion that the artist is sick because he is trying to plead double jeopardy, saying because they said he did it before and was not prosecuted, they cannot try to charge him with the same crime now, although the charges are not based on old events but current infractions. He believes that the artist is ill in the head because he has been dating underage girls for years, but now he is saying that he is fighting for his life. That man's point was that the artist is trying to use his fame and status to vindicate himself. Another person chimed in and described his illness as demonic. They also brought up the privilege of other superstars, including Michael Jackson, and the displaced loyalty of some mothers to the spotlight and money, allowing their children to spend the night at a grown man's house without them.

An important discussion concerning one's perspective contributed greatly to the discussion and purpose of the project. People were answering some of the survey questions from the perspective of never having experienced certain occurrences. Many, however, eventually grasped the point of seeing the violation from the perspective of the violated, acknowledging the need for the church to respond appropriately and without judgment, respectfully empathizing with someone else who has experienced violations.

This night of discussion included various areas of importance that informed and contributed to the increase of awareness of the extended effects of sexual or physical violence on persons. In the end, one of the women shared her volatile experience, as well as how the evening really ministered to her: the service, the sermon, the discussion, and the people. She shared how her therapist and friend just died, and so she was not going to come, but she was encouraged that night and was grateful she came and did not stay home. She also stressed how important it is to connect with a professional counselor. After her deep disclosure and sharing of her experience, we embraced one another and prayed for each other for healing, encouragement, the transformation in the church's and participants' awareness, to break the silence, embrace others, give affirmation and love to one another and to those who feel ostracized and are alone, sharing the real love of God with those who seem to need it the most.

CHAPTER FIVE

Reflections, Summary of Results, and Conclusion

> "The spirit of the Lord God is upon me, because the Lord has anointed me; he has sent me to bring good news to the oppressed, to bind up the brokenhearted, to proclaim liberty to the captives, and release to the prisoners; to proclaim the year of the Lord's favor..."[73]

Reflections

One of the women in the church who participated in this research project made an extremely profound statement, which I have decided to embrace. This statement is connected to the thematic scripture of my research project and call to do this project. She began by saying, "I know and have already accepted *God's* success in your life," she continued with this statement that took me aback: "you are *the voice for broken women*...and [you] will have successful ministry." To be regarded as the "voice" for broken women was very emotional for me. As one who has experienced sexual molestation and been directly affected by physical/domestic violence, one who seemed to lose her voice but who has recently rediscovered it, it is amazing to now use my voice to "proclaim liberty" through the transformative preached Word of

---

[73] Isaiah 61:1–2a.

God. It is also amazing because, when I was first called by God to preach, I was sure that no one would want to hear what I had to say. Obviously, this argument has been muted. Praise God!

For many years, I suffered from low self-esteem but success-fully disguised it with the boldness of the authority vested in me as a corrections officer. Regardless, I lived in crippling fear as a result of having been molested. This led to making decisions out of fear, some good and some bad. Nonetheless, fear was a factor in those decisions. Fear caused me to speak up and be quiet; both led to me being ostracized, rejected, ridiculed, and persecuted. I understand what it feels like to live feeling excluded, unworthy, less than others, unable to embrace the fullness of love; looking in the mirror and never seeing me for me but seeing myself the way I thought others perceived me. I also saw a distorted image of my body because of what I was made to feel at a young age, being forced to show my little body to a teenage boy and his little brothers. I remained quiet out of fear, fear reinforced by retaliation in the violent killing of my pet rabbit, instigated by my abuser after I attempted to speak out.

Throughout my years of education, I continued to feel less than, inadequate, and unequal. It was not until 2018 that I actually felt as though I was worthy to be in the same class with my peers and that I could contribute substantially to the cohort and all that was to come. During this journey, my classmates had no idea of my feelings and self-projected inadequacies until I orally presented a prophetic preaching assignment that spoke to social justice issues of the rape of men and women. My portion of that project focused on campus rape of women. It was then that I disclosed, for the first time publicly, the failed attempt of a friend to date rape me using a drug called Rohypnol, also known as "roofies." During that presentation, I sobbed and was vulnerable to my classmates. My classmates, "The Remnant," embraced me, showed me love and compassion, and affirmed me, the same way we all did for each other since our journey began in January 2017. The effectiveness of transformational preaching began the moment I entered into the Doctor of Ministry program through my professors and the loving and influential support of my cohort family. My voice, along with the voices of my classmates, became an asset, shaping all of us for the ministry that is to follow. For me, it is this work through this research project that has made me the "*voice for broken women*."

Through the voices of the various feminist and womanist theologians who contributed to my research project, I continued to rediscover and shape my voice and identity. For the majority of my life, I was educated in predominantly White school systems. Schools, at that time, failed to celebrate and acknowledge the differences of Black students, our culture, and our voices. It was not until college that I began to learn about Black history and the phenomenal impact Black people had in the making and progress of America. As an African-American woman preacher, I have experienced sexism in the pulpit from various church leaders, both male and female, although I was nurtured by a pastor who was not only inclusive but also supportive of women who are called to preach. He was also very protective of us, safeguarding us from pitfalls that were not recognizable to us as women, and he also shielded us from unnecessary church hurts that could be avoided.

The resources I used increased my awareness of the diversity of females, our voices, influences, impacts, and the absence of our voices. As I began researching various sources to inform my project, I began with the resources I normally use; various well-respected commentaries that are very good; however, incomplete—meaning, not exhaustive. These resources were not comprehensive because they only recorded one voice and one perspective, which is primarily the White patriarchal voice that co-signs the normative Western European biblical interpretations of the pericopes. As I explored and preached, particularly the stories of Tamar, the unnamed concubine, and Dinah, I noticed that the voices of these women were silenced. Yes, Tamar expressed her displeasure at her rape and pleaded with her brother to not violate her. The story is then interpreted through and focused on the responses and actions of the males in her life. Not many, if any, of the traditional commentaries or resources that I had valued included the perspective of the victimized women, introduced the lenses of people of color, or suggested the fact that these offenses against these women were morally wrong. Some of the participants in the research study spoke to the fact that the Bible gives so many accounts of these abuses. They were situations perceived and written as the norm for how women were and are to be regarded and treated. Many traditional biblical commentaries neglect to comment on, address, or bring awareness to the mental, physical, and emotional effects the women sustained as a result of sexism, racism, patriarchy, and politics.

Given my responsibility to preach four specific scriptures that graphically record shameful and demeaning defilements against the women whose stories these are, it was necessary to lend my voice to the hushed and broken bodies of these despoiled women. The resources cited in my literature review, which were provided by a few of the prominent womanist and feminist theologians and pastoral caregivers helped me to hear, shape, and echo the voices of these women. In speaking on behalf of these women, I rediscovered my own voice, and I was empowered. As I preached in all of my femininity, an anointed woman preacher wearing stiletto heels, conveying the embodiment of the female biblical characters, the debasement of the abuses, and the need for these women to be heard became my imperative. I needed to imprint their images on the consciousness of the congregants.

Another important resource, written from a different lens, is *True to Our Native Land*, an African-American New Testament commentary written by African-American theologians.[74] This commentary also contains articles that lend the homiletical and hermeneutical expertise of Black preachers and Black biblical scholars. This source broadened my understanding through relevant interpretations that incorporated the Black experience through the lens of African-American men and women. One of the prominent articles for me that was instrumental to this project gave a unique perspective. Suffering Black women perceive Jesus to be intertwined with them as co-suffer. However, Jesus bears the brunt of the load while they are suffering. Another source that is inclusive is, *They Were All Together in One Place? Toward Minority Biblical Criticism,*[75] proffers commentary to some of the Old Testament texts from the perspective of various minorities.

There is one resource I regret not exploring, the *African American Heritage Bible.* [76] It may have been informative concerning the perspective of a Black interpretation of the pericopes that I had explored. However, like other traditional study Bibles, I am not sure if it would have significantly offered a womanist perspective and voice. Unfortunately, some African-American men, in some imperious ways, have also been contaminated and influenced negatively by the White patriarchal perspective, voice, and dominance. However, many have fallen prey to the subjugation of

---

[74] Blount, Brian K., gen.ed. , Cain Hope Felder, Clarice J. Martin, and Emerson B. Powery, assoc. eds. True to Our Native Land: An African American New Testament Commentary. Minnapolis: Fortress Press, 2007.

[75] Bailey, Randall C. , Tat-siong Benney Liew, and Fernando F. Segovia, eds. They Were All Together in One Place?: Toward Minority Biblical Criticism. Atlanta: Society of Biblical Literature, 2009.

[76] Felder, Cain Hope. The Original African American Heritage Bible. Valley Forge: Judson Press, 1993.

"slave mentality," even when preaching and teaching the Holy Word of God, which is liberating.[77]

> Don't forget you must pitch the young Black male against the old Black male. ..You must use the dark skin slaves versus the light skin slaves...You must use the female versus the male. ..You must also have your white servants and over-seers distrust all Blacks, but it is necessary that your slaves trust and depend on us. They must love, respect, and trust only us.[78]

> Whether Lynch existed or not is unimportant. Whoever it was, the true author of this strategy was right in his approach for the continuing servitude of blacks and in establishing a slave mentality in our race. All that was subject to change is exactly who the master is at any given time. [79]

The "new master" is silence, and the oppressed are women. This mentality, inclusive of all humanity, has contributed greatly to the lack of awareness and guilty silence in the church regarding sexual and physical abuse against women. This deafening silence is not just a contagion in one particular denomination; it is an

---

[77] Jackson, Kevin. "American Thinker." https://www.americanthinker.com . June 15, 2010. https://www.americanthinker.com/articles/2010/06/the_slave_mentality.html#ix-zz5ipm8LnAF (accessed March 21, 2019).

[78] Jackson, Kevin.

[79] Jackson, Kevin

infectious contagion within the *majority* of the universal Church that confesses and professes Jesus as Lord. [80]

Initially, this project was going to focus more on women who have experienced these abuses, which was a very broad approach to the issues. This subject matter is very provocative, and the risk of possibly re-injuring or re-victimizing participants was great. The Human Subjects Resource Committee expressed this concern. It helped to guide me in a direction that would be of minimal risk and still address the issues of abuse against women. Their observations also helped me to more sharply focus and fine-tune my initial idea and pinpoint my passion and what it was that I desired to accomplish. This was frustrating. In the process of re-evaluating the best method for approaching this topic, I came to the realization that I was trying to put the cart before the horse. By nature, I am a protector and fixer. I came to the realization that I cannot "fix" this epidemic alone. It became clear that the church would be the best place to start for advocating, addressing, and being effective in helping women who have been sexually and physically abused. In my initial proposal, bringing awareness and breaking the silence of the church concerning these abuses were goals that were to be accomplished through the project. The shift was beneficial and instrumental in putting the cart in its rightful place, behind the horse. Confronting the church about its years of silence and lack of support and addressing the systemic issues that contribute to the maltreatment of women needed to be preached from the pulpit. The pulpit represents the place of godly authority and influence. This provoked a response from the church that allowed women who have been victimized to be acknowledged and affirmed by the

---

[80] Science, Religion, and Culture Harvard Divinity School. The implying of the "majority" is informed by a survey conducted of 1,000 random Protestant pastors. Utilizing these results as the scale, they would likely yield confirmation of the enormous number of churches that are silent about, barely responsive and non-responsive to the urgency of addressing these issues.

very institution they trust to give them hope, which is the church. The dismantling of the church's silence has become the foundation for continuing the work of advocating on behalf of women who have and are presently experiencing sexual and physical abuses.

There are a few things that I would have done differently during the process of the project. One major change would have been to write a reflection on each sermon immediately after it was preached, which was my intent, but it did not happen. One contributing factor that prohibited me from immediately writing was the exhaustion I experienced after preaching. The subject matter was sensitive, intense, important, and violent. Preaching sermons of this nature required me to embody the sermon and the character so that the congregation would be drawn into the experience to gain a better understanding of the violations and respond to the call to action that went forth. It was very draining emotionally, physically, and mentally; my body required rest. Initially, the implementation of the project was to be for six to eight weeks. These four weeks proved to be sufficiently effective. The project may have been almost too difficult had it been longer in duration. Although this was taxing, I would do it all over again.

The focus group was limited to fifteen participants. Those who were in the group were the first to sign up; however, there were others who wanted to join in but were unable to because of the size restriction. Increasing the focus group from fifteen to twenty is something I would consider changing in hindsight. Also, having a congregational group discussion after the last sermon or as a closing session the following week would have been a better way to close the congregation's participation in the project. The congregation did not have the same opportunity as the core group did to express their experiences, ask questions, or offer beneficial criticism. One person inquired what she was to do with all this new and enlightening information and all her questions. She asked if there would be a Bible study follow-up in the future or a way to express how she was affected by the sermons. She then mentioned she should have signed up for the core group when she had the chance. Responses like these inform me how to further proceed in continuing this work.

The last reflection was somewhat troublesome. A comment was made that caused me to re-evaluate my approach of how I prefaced one of the sermons. I struggled with whether I could have given the congregation a better indication of the graphic nature in the role-playing of Tamar in the sermon, "Can't You Hear Her?" I had given what I thought was a detailed explanation of the process and meaning of an incarnational translation, but it was not enough for a couple of the attendees. I am not totally convinced that I should have informed the audience differently. One participant said it was very shocking, and she was not prepared for the scene. She continued to say if she could have been forewarned in more detail, she could have had the choice to leave the sanctuary during the enactment of Tamar's rape. However, this same individual that had never experienced any form of abuse revealed that the visual display gave her a different perspective of what victims of rape experience. With her words in mind, I judge this method of preaching to be transformative, very effective, and able to do what it needed to accomplish. Although it was shocking and uncomfortable, it increased the awareness and need for the church to break the silence of sexual and physical violence against women.

Summary of Results

Congregational surveys before and after the sermon series were used to measure the knowledge of the participants, their willingness to break the silence of the church, and their views and understanding (or lack thereof) of biblical accounts of and their views of God in sexual and physical abuses against women. Lastly, they measured whether listeners identify these issues as worldwide social justice issues with impact on not only women, but the preservation of all humanity. The pre and post surveys did not have the capability to efficiently measure and compare the results. The results of these pre and post surveys did not illustrate a significant shift, neither an increase nor a decrease, in answers to many of the questions that were given. The reason for a lack of shift in the results is believed to be the wording used in both the pre and post surveys. The questions that were asked on both surveys were exactly the same in their wording and structure, and appeared to lack in clarity. The assumption is reconstructing questions two, five, and ten in the pre and post questions, and post question eight would have provided optimum clarity in its understanding and intent. This may have better informed the answers selected. Therefore, it is possible that it might have generated results that would have enabled significant measurements of any differences. The measured results could have determined through the pre and post congregational surveys how the transformational sermon series affected them, and if there was a shift in the congregation's awareness to embrace the need to break the silence in the church and increase their knowledge of the character of God in conjunction with the violent scriptures that were preached.

By contrast, the focus group's participation, evaluations, comments, and actions confirmed their growing understanding of the importance of affirming, embracing, and lending emotional support to women who have had or may now be having these volatile abominations against them. The sharing by members of the focus group provided confirmation that the sermons were impactful and life-altering. The data generated from the weekly congregation and weekly focus group surveys was measured and yielded positive and supportive results, which prove that I have achieved the intended goals and purpose of my research project. As the researcher, I successfully created sermons from texts that record brutal attacks that violate women and are rarely preached. Through the use of transformational preaching, transformation occurred in the congregation.

This transformative sermon series is homiletically unique because it effectively used an amalgamation of preaching methods to address difficult subject matter. The multiplicity of methods that were used in this project was intentional. These methods were prophetic, incarnational translation, expository (a combination of both inductive and deductive), and narrative. Although there are sermon series that have been preached utilizing a combination of intertwined methods, I am not aware of and have not experienced sermons with these specific methods and order. It was important to begin with the Old Testament prophetic passage by the prophet Isaiah. Prophetic preaching confronts social justice issues that affect today's society at large, outside of the walls of the church. It speaks truth to power and gives voice to the oppressed and disheartened. Prophetic preaching provides a vision of a better world and confronts the powers in this world that would stand in the way of that vision. It also demands accountability and response from leaders who influence our immediate realm (the church), and self.

Opening the project series with Isaiah 61:1–3, the prophetic sermon, "The Time Is Now," opened the door to preaching freely versus preaching fearfully or not at all about controversial issues.[81] Preaching freely is preaching boldly about difficult topics, such as betrayal and intimate abuse, which are taboo subjects in the church. It enables the preacher to proclaim God's Word unapologetically, standing firm on one's credence. Conversely, preaching fearfully gives control to the anticipation of negative judgment of those who may be offended, and it limits the preacher's ability to

---

[81] Sermon manuscript in Appendix F, pages 161 ff.

preach truth to power outside of his or her comfort level in faith. When preaching truth about issues that have been hushed by the church and are affecting the quality of life for some congregants, it will offend some, make many uneasy, anger some, and yet give freedom to others.

The Isaiah sermon issued a charge and a clarion call to the church about its responsibility to the oppressed as mandated by God. It provided important and even startling statistics of sexual and physical abuses against women, the lack of the church's and leaders' responses, and pointed out the neglect of women in our congregations that have and are contending with these abuses. It was important to paint a picture for the congregation, through the preached word, for them to see the severity of this issue, the need to learn about it, and the need to no longer be unaware, silent, and dismissive. This sermon set the stage for what was to come in the following weeks. The congregation knew about the existence of sexual and physical abuses, but needed a transformation in their attitudes and lack of responses to the issues. This sermon also confronted the congregation with God's disappointment in their ignoring the plight of the "least of these," the abused. The sermon gave hope to all. It gave hope to the abused. It gave hope to the congregation by allowing them to accept the challenge to correct their lack of affirmation of abused women and gave them the ability to now respond effectively, empowered with the love of God. It also gave hope to the preacher to acknowledge that the time is now for this project, this sermon, and for this preacher to embrace her voice and anointing. This sermon brought forth a greater awareness of abuses against women, the importance of the church's response, and a broader definition of and perspective on abuse, both as a social justice issue and the expectations of God.

After the prophetic call for awareness, the rape of Tamar was preached through the proposed lens of Tamar in today's context using an incarnational translation method of preaching. The sermon, "Can't You Hear Her?"[82] from 1 Samuel 13:1–22, gave a real-life example of the traumatic event of the rape from the view of the victim. This sermon was intense. The Scripture became embodied in the flesh (incarnated), and brought to life in the form of a realistic contemporary role-play. This biblical re-enactment in today's multicultural context drew the congregation into the experience that rape victims innocently incur and the perpetrators they know, love, and trust. It also drew attention to the worldwide incursion of this invasive act into every nation, race, and culture. There were women in the congregation who relived the moment of trying to escape by running from their assailants. In running from them, it caused some to run to drugs. However, during the preaching moment, it was not possible to run out of the church toward drugs; they were compelled to run to God instead. Seeking and finding communion in this way was very powerful and pivotal. It began personal healing in some, influenced the lives of others, and its impact continues to reverberate as they share.

Using the incarnational technique, this sermon also began breaking the silence, not only for the congregation at large but also for victimized women in the congregation. The voice of the victimized woman in the Bible through the woman preacher is heard clearly, a voice that had been devalued and dismissed because of ingrained patriarchy. This voice spoke for women through the ages who have been and continue to be tormented, demoralized, hushed, overlooked, and discriminated against by classism, sexism, and racism, and silenced embodied in an overwhelmingly patriarchal society. Overall, preaching this sermon drew the congregation into a relationship with the Word, the God of the Bible, and the God of their lives, and revealed how this correlation is fruitful for spiritual and temporal life.

---

[82] Sermon manuscript in Appendix F, pages 172 ff.

This was a very heartrending sermon. My father was troubled by it. It was too much for him to bear. After its delivery, he was speechless, and it brought him to tears to have to witness such an enactment and to come to an understanding of what women endure at the hands of batterers/abusers. He had intended to support me in this endeavor but admitted he could not handle it. He said he could not put into words how he felt and did not want to talk about it. He did not attend the last two services. While the blending of the biblical text, a contemporary role-play, and the exploration of the victim's quieted account of the episode had its effect on my hearers, it encouraged me to delve into womanist theology and hermeneutical resources to hear what was not spoken. This contributed to my development into a womanist theologian.

A combination of both the inductive and deductive movements was purposeful in the formation of the sermon on Judges 19, which chronicles the violent gang rape of the unnamed concubine. The sermon was entitled, "The Absence of the Presence of God. "[83] This sermon addressed not only the gang rape of the unnamed concubine, but also marital relations and the relationship between fathers and daughters. The deductive approach presented the issue and its assumed cause, and the inductive proved the assumption. The overarching assumption is the absence of the presence of God resulted in various violations, abuses, and broken relationships within this pericope. Inductively, the issue was presented in a manner that did not alienate the audience but presented them with real-life experiences occurring today and need to be addressed. It proved that the violent acts of today are a result of the absence of the true presence of God in the hearts of humankind, and in these particular instances, the hearts of men.

The incarnational sermon that was preached the week before allowed the congregation to vicariously see and experience

[83] Sermon manuscript in Appendix F, pages 187 ff.

victimization. The combination of the inductive and deductive this week allowed the congregation to understand and acknowledge the root of the experienced abuse. It also presented current events in a manner that portrayed the darkness of one's heart and the result thereof. One of the greatest results of this sermon methodology was the shift in the congregation's perspective of how God did or did not play a role in violence. In the questionnaire, some presumed the Bible supports violence toward women. After this sermon, in discussion, many revealed they now understood the violence in the Scriptures differently, and the Bible is not supporting the violence but merely exposing it. Some women who were victims revealed they had blamed God and believed God was responsible for their abuse. Now that they have experienced this sermon, these women reported no longer blaming God and no longer being angry with God, but fully giving fault and blame to their abusers alone. This was a great victory, not only for their psyche healing but in freeing them to begin healing and growing spiritually. As previously stated, concerning this sermon, I felt as though I had betrayed the woman in this story. But after hearing about the effectiveness of this sermon due to the layering of multiple homiletical methods in preparation for preaching, I was encouraged and stretched. I was drawn beyond my level of comfort, expectation, and understanding of the effectiveness of using the combination of the inductive and deductive styles for this pericope. The combination yielded different yet affirming results while maintaining the integrity of the text.

Last to be incorporated was the use of a narrative sermon. The use of the narrative method of preaching was to compel the congregation to share in Dinah's experience in the sermon, "What's Love Got to Do with It?"[84] A narrative was created to influence the congregation to reflect on their own life experiences with violated

---

[84] Sermon manuscript in Appendix F, pages 195 ff.

love so they might share in and identify with Dinah's experiences. Through the narrative, the congregation was immediately presented with the conflict, the misuse of love by men in Dinah's life. From there, they were led to see the greater picture of abuse in the name of love. The connecting of the congregants' experience to Dinah's and further to the experience of women who have been sexually and physically violated, created empathy and a greater understanding of the seriousness of the issues involved and the need for them to be addressed. These issues included privilege, cultural differences, coercion, and various types of discrimination, all which are shared conflicts in the pericope and lives of the congregants. The narrative then shifted and began to unfold how this situation impacts the individual and gives a command to respond through the Word of God. Jesus gave the world two specific commandments, to love God, and to love each other as we love ourselves. Love was the premise for the sermon. The congregation was propelled into immediate action as the people of God who are to love *all* as commanded by God, and how they are to transfer this love through the breaking of the silence, heightening one's own awareness, and sharing with others to enlighten their awareness. In doing so, the church progresses in its efforts to destroy the systemic evils (sexism, racism, and classism) that contribute to sexual and physical abuses against women.

In conclusion, this sermon series began with the prophetic. It prophetically proclaimed the social issue, that is, sexual and physical violence against women, and the need for the church to be aware of its severity and to respond, no longer being silent about the issue. Then, using incarnational translation, an explicit demonstration of the brutality experienced by violated women was shared to heighten the awareness of the congregation and give an understanding of the severity of abuse. Next, the congregation was further introduced through the inductive/deductive styles to the systemic nature of the abuse and how the systemic root of evil is woven into the fabric of our world. It also spoke to the evil in the hearts of men because God was not truly present in their hearts. And lastly, the use of the narrative style of preaching connected the congregation to the plight of all abused women by allowing them to identify with them and reflect on their own experience of violation. Hence, the congregation was no longer looking from the outside in, but were now a part of the experience, which heightened their awareness, brought them to a place of affirming abused women, and speaking out against such violence. The order of the sermons was strategically planned to bring the congregation from awareness to action. It proved to be effective. It is my opinion that this combination as a sermon series will be very effective and valuable for preaching about other controversial issues that are sensitive, difficult, and considered to be a taboo in the church. Most importantly, it will be transformational and will produce positive and life-altering results within individuals and the body of Christ.

Preaching transformational sermons increased the levels of the congregation's awareness, awakened their consciousness, and influenced the need for change. The silence of the congregation, lack of empathy, and unresponsiveness to sexual and physical abuse against women were dismantled. Lastly, a platform was created to preach, discuss, and study transformative sermons about uncomfortable and formidable scriptures chosen to address difficult subject matter that needs a response from the church.

A major result of this study that is not measurable through surveys and not included as an intentional result is the healing that has taken place as a result of this research. There were several women who stated that this project has helped start their personal healing, has given them a voice, and has begun healing their personal relationship with and understanding of God. As an example, one woman from the congregation credited her budding sobriety and no longer choosing drugs but choosing God instead to the incarnational translation method of preaching Tamar's story in "Can't You Hear Her?" Not only is she sober as a result but also is enrolling in a Christian college to study psychology and counseling. She may now share her story with other women who have been victimized, affirming them, letting them know that God loves them, and asserting that healing through the Word of God is possible.

Conclusion

This journey, which I have had the pleasure and, I have been told, the boldness to embark upon, has been a transformative life experience. It has been enlightening, meaningful, powerful, and empowering, which is just the beginning. The purpose of the project was to use transformational preaching to cause a transformation in the congregation's awareness and break the silence. Not only did a transformation occur in the congregants but a transformation has also occurred within me. There is a phrase that is commonly coined: the sermon is first to the preacher and then to the pew. This has been apparent throughout the sermon series and in the experience gained.

This research study has come to an end as a project, but it has now become the springboard for furthering the ministry work. The participants of this study have become the nucleus and will be instrumental in informing other congregants of the importance to advocate on behalf of the many who are victimized by sexual and physical/domestic abuses, and the need for the church to respond affirmatively and break the silence. As a result of this research project, this church can influence other churches to participate in informational workshops that provide awareness of domestic violence and rape. In addition, the church can effectively provide tools to assist those in need, become familiar with and partner with help agencies in the area, assist in making connections with various counseling professionals for those in need, and create confidential spaces for discussions that assist and affirm victims.

During the discussions, a concern was expressed about children's inability to have space to process their experience in a non-aggressive manner. Mainly because many are forced to keep silent about the abuse, the need to be inclusive of the children of domestic violence was mentioned. Some of the help agencies that attended the services have already acknowledged their prior efforts and current desire to partner with churches. One representative believed the approach was unconventional but very effective and has expressed the desire to continue working together in this arena.

The church secretary was moved by the need and importance of this issue, so much so, that she recently asked me if there was training that would teach her how to answer a call should someone in distress call the church. I was deeply moved by her willingness to learn how to respond. I gave her the information about one of the agencies that provides training. As a retort, she told me to go for the training and then come back to train her and others. I believe I have just received my next assignment in this work. My pastor is very supportive and encouraging. He has been a valuable asset throughout the process and upholds the importance of speaking and acting against sexual and physical abuses. He also believes in affirming those who have had these experiences, as well as protecting others from these abuses. Because of his conviction to this issue, I believe when I approach him, he will respond favorably to the church becoming an integral part of the cause, and will encourage pursuing partnerships with help agencies that provide further training for leaders, church personnel, and members to assist those in despairing situations.

Because transformation has begun within the leadership of the church, in the congregation, and in individuals, there is now a need for the church to continue to move forward. This can be accomplished by continuing to stand for ending the silence and bringing awareness of sexual and physical violence against women throughout the universal church. Some initial steps to move this congregation forward are to:

- Create a zero-tolerance policy to be incorporated into the church's constitution and by-laws, for all clergy and ministry leaders regarding sexual and physical violence within the community, the church, and the home. This policy is to be signed by all current clergy and ministry leaders, and annually by newly-appointed or elected leaders prior to assuming a leadership position within the church.
- Provide all leadership and staff with training to receive and respond positively to the concerns of those who may be seeking emergency assistance through local domestic violence or rape crisis and intervention agencies.
- Provide the congregation with educational and informational materials of local crisis and intervention agencies that are in the community. Make the information available to all by posting and displaying in designated areas.
- Partner with local agencies, beginning with 180° Turning Lives Around, the Mercy Center–Family Resource Center, Covenant House, and Catholic Charities (Monmouth and Ocean Counties). Partnering with these agencies will provide training for clergy, leaders, and the congregations, as well as workshops and forums to be extended to the community and area churches.
- Incorporate sermons concerning sexual and physical violence, particularly during Domestic Violence Awareness

and Sexual Assault Awareness months.[85, 86] In addition, to institute Bible studies about these abuses and to study the Scriptures that have been manipulated to support and validate abuse, discrimination, and oppression of women.

- Lastly, address the accountability of abusers/batterers through sermons and Bible studies.

Although I may not be exactly sure of what the future holds for me, one thing I am sure of: *the time is now!* God has anointed, prepared, and called me for such a time as this, to be the "*voice for broken women.*" Some of my aspirations are to:

- Continue working with my pastor and church to move forward.
- Create a curriculum for heightening awareness, breaking the silence, and addressing sexual and physical violence against women and other severe issues through transformative sermons in the church.
- Present this approach to various denominational associations and conventions, cultures, and nations worldwide, teaching the created curriculum and need for bringing awareness and breaking the silence.
- Form alliances with various sexual and physical violence prevention, awareness, and help agencies on local, national, and international levels, both secular and ecumenical.

---

[85] October is Domestic Violence Awareness Month. April is Sexual Assault Awareness Month.

[86] The Center for Family Justice: Statistics. n.d. https://centerforfamilyjustice. org (accessed January 17, 2019).

I am committed to proclaiming the fullness of God's Word with the fervor and intentionality of transformational preaching, preaching that provokes response and transforms lives.

Curriculum Vitae

EDUCATION

NEW BRUNSWICK THEOLOGICAL SEMINARY,
New Brunswick, New Jersey
Doctor of Ministry: Transformational Preaching. 2019
Honor: 2018-2019 Koops Memorial Academic Scholarship
- Master of Divinity 2011
- International Student Stollenbosh University, South Africa

UNIVERSITY OF PHOENIX, Phoenix, Arizona
B. S. Business Administration 2006

OCEAN COUNTY COLLEGE, Toms River, NJ,
A. S. Business Administration

MINISTERIAL EXPERIENCE

Second Baptist Church, Asbury Park, NJ- 2013 – present. Associate Pastor and spiritual leader. Coordinator of the Christian Board of Education Ministry.

Second Baptist Church of Toms River, South Toms River, NJ–2001-2016. Assistant to Pastor. Youth ministries and Sunday school.

Director and organizer for the Community Vacation Bible School and staff.

New York Theological Seminary, NY 2017–present. Adjunct Professor for the Certificate Program in Christian Ministry.

Triumphed Covenant House of Prayer, New Brunswick, NJ–2008 – 2016

Pilgrim Baptist Church, Red Bank, NJ,–2006–2013 *Haiti Missions Outreach Ministry*- active & on-site participant.

MEMBERSHIP IN PROFESSIONAL AND COMMUNITY ORGANIZATIONS

Nation Council of Negro Women North Shore Area Section, President

Improved Benevolent Protective Order of Elks of the World, Grand Assistant Chaplain

Maggie G. Hill Temple # 1308 Toms River, NJ, Vice Daughter Ruler

New Jersey State Daughters of Elk, State Chaplain.

Eastern Division Antler Guard, I.B. P. Order of Elks, Division Chaplain.

New Jersey State Police Benevolent Association, Local #240, Monmouth County, Freehold, NJ since 1990. Retired.

Covenant Team Members

Gary Michael Bailey, Sr. Gary's life motto is "Every accomplishment starts with the decision to try." He has a Bachelor's Degree in Business Management from Montclair State College. Additionally, he has a Master of Arts in Criminal Justice from Shelbourne University, graduating Magna Cum Laude. He is a member of Phi Beta Sigma Fraternity, Inc. Gary is an exceptional team player with strong analytical and organizational skills. Lastly, Gary serves as Chairman of the Trustee Ministry at Mount Olive Baptist Church, Plainfield, NJ.

Jaikia R. Fair. She was educated in the Toms River, New Jersey School systems graduating from Toms River High School East in 2006. Jaikia attended Johnson C. Smith University in Charlotte, NC, a HBCU. She received her Bachelor of Science in Health Education/ Community Health. Jaikia is seeking a career as an interpreter for the hearing impaired. Jaikia is a member at Bethel Community Church Intl., in Neptune, New Jersey. She serves on the Praise and Worship ministry as an anointed psalmist.

Ernestine Counts. Ernestine Counts is currently employed with the Division of Child Protection and Permanency, formerly known as the Division of Youth and Family Services and has worked there for 20 years. She is presently the supervisor of the Adolescent Unit and is a strong advocate for adolescents and enjoys working with adolescents. Her academic achievements include a Bachelor of Science degree with a distinction in Social Work from Stockton University and a master's in social work from Monmouth University. Ernestine worships at New Hope Baptist Church in Toms River, serving as president of the Usher Board Ministry.

Glenn Johnson. Glenn was born, raised and educated in the Newark, New Jersey public school system. While attending the New Jersey Institute of Technology in New Jersey as an Engineering major, he became a member Phi Beta Sigma Fraternity. Before completing his degree, he was recruited to become a NJ State Trooper. During his service as a New Jersey State Trooper, he achieved the status of Detective. He is a war veteran, having served in the armed forces as a Staff Sergeant in the United States Air Force. Currently he is employed as Train Conductor for New Jersey Transit. Glenn is a member of Franklin St. John United Methodist Church in Newark, New Jersey.

Desiree Pendleton. Desiree was born, raised and educated in Lakewood, New Jersey. She attended Rider University achieving a Bachelor of Arts Degree in Psychology. She has experience in the psychology field, including working as a Counselor/Teacher in the Social Service field (Group Homes for Female Adolescents and Autistic Women, Inpatient Psychiatric Hospital (Geriatrics), and Psychiatric Crisis). She has a master's degree in business administration, changing career fields (from Psychology to Business). She is as a civilian employee for the military, Navy, as a Contracts Specialist at the MDL Joint Base in Lakehurst, New Jersey.

Kerwin Webb. Minister Webb earned his Bachelor of Science degree in Business Administration from Alabama State University in Montgomery, Alabama with a concentration in Finance. He is currently matriculating in the Master of Divinity Program at Princeton Theological Seminary. He has earned a Certificate in Christian Ministry from Pillar College in NJ. Presently, he serves as Pastor of Youth Ministry at Second Baptist Church in Asbury Park, NJ. He is the founder of the RMW Foundation, Inc. , a non-profit organization for youth and young adults to provide educational assistance, tutoring, mentoring, community development, investment, and spiritual development and guidance.

Jenell Jackson, LCSW. Jennell Jackson is a Licensed Clinical Social Worker who helps individuals navigate daily life stressors. She believes in meeting the client where they are to help them go further than they think is possible. Before starting Jackson Counseling Services, LLC, Jennell spent eight of her twelve years as a therapist working for the United States government. After a successful career of helping veterans who were returning from war, she now empowers the hearts and minds of a multifaceted clientele throughout the diversities of life. Jennell enjoys working with and providing individual and couple therapy. Her versatility allows her to provide counseling online to clients.

Informed Consultants

Raynard Smith, Ph.D. is the Associate Professor of Pastoral Care/Pastoral Theology at New Brunswick Theological Seminary in New Brunswick, New Jersey. He is currently chair of the Ministry Studies Department and oversees the Master of Arts in Pastoral Care and Counseling program. He has a Ph.D. in Psychology and Religion from Drew University; Master of Divinity and Master of Theology degrees from Princeton Theological Seminary. He has several years of experience as a certified chaplain and pastoral counselor working in the hospital, hospice, and medical clinic contexts.

Danielle L. Hunter, D. Min., is an Itinerant Elder in the African Methodist Episcopal Church, presently serving as pastor of Bethel A. M.E. Church, Asbury Park, New Jersey. During her 25 years of ministry, in addition to pastoring, Rev. Hunter has been privileged to serve as a chaplain in the following areas: hospital, hospice, nursing facility and prison chaplaincy. In February 2018, she was appointed Dean of the A. M.E. Church New Jersey Conference Ministerial Institute. She has been a member of the A. M.E. Church New Jersey Conference Board of Examiners. She has a Bachelor of Arts degree in sociology and a certificate in criminology from Douglass College (Rutgers University); a Master of Divinity degree from New Brunswick Theological Seminary; and a Doctor of Ministry degree from the Theological School of Drew University.

Semaj Y. Vanzant, Sr., D. Min., graduated Magna Cum Laude, earning a Bachelor of Arts degree in Political Science and Minor in Psychology from Gannon University, Erie, Pennsylvania, a Master of Divinity degree from Princeton Theological Seminary, Princeton, New Jersey, and his Doctor of Ministry from St. Paul's School of Theology, Oklahoma City, Oklahoma. Pastor Vanzant is currently serving as the pastor-teacher at Second Baptist Church of Asbury Park, New Jersey.

Traci C. West, Ph.D. , is Professor of Ethics and African American Studies at Drew Theological School in Madison, New Jersey. She received her BA from Yale University (New Haven, CT), her MDiv. from Pacific School of Religion (Berkeley, CA), and her PhD from Union Theological Seminary (New York, New York). She is the author of *Disruptive Christian Ethics: When Racism and Women's Lives Matter* (Westminster John Knox Press, 2006), *Wounds of the Spirit: Black Women, Violence, and Resistance Ethics* (New York University Press, 1999), and the editor of *Our Family Values: Same-sex Marriage and Religion* (Praeger, 2006). She has also written several articles on violence against women, racism, clergy ethics, sexuality and other justice issues in church and society. She is an ordained elder in the New York Annual Conference of the United Methodist Church.

Survey Questionnaires

Pre-Survey Questionnaire

1. How do you rate the importance of the church addressing the issue of sexual violence against women from the pulpit?

    a. Very Relevant

    b. Relevant

    c. Somewhat Relevant

    d. Not relevant

2. My level of awareness of the pandemic of sexual and physical violence is:

    a. Excellent

    b. Good

    c. Fair

    d. Low

3. What percentage of women in your congregation would you estimate have experienced sexual and or physical (domestic included) violence?

    a. Less than 5%

    b. 6-10%

    c. 11-20%

    d. 21-30%

    e. 31-40%

    f. 41-50%

    g. Greater than 50%

    h. I don't know

4. I have been exposed to sermons that speak to the sexual and physical abuses of women

    a. Never

    b. Rarely

    c. Often

    d. Regularly

5. My level of reception of preaching sermons in the church concerning sexual and physical abuse is:

    a. Excellent

    b. Good

    c. Fair

    d. Low

    e. Additional comments if applicable:

6. It is important for the congregation and its leadership to join together for action and advocacy to end the silence around sexual and physical violence against women:

    a. Agree

    b. Somewhat agree

    c. Disagree

7. How likely are you willing to participate in discussions surrounding sexual and physical abuses of women that worship in your church?

   a. Most-likely

   b. Likely

   c. Somewhat likely

   d. Not likely

8. Those who have experienced a form of sexual or physical abuse should remain silent and get over it:

   a. Strongly agree

   b. Agree

   c. Disagree

   d. Strongly disagree

9. Women that have been victimized usually are silent and do not seek assistance because of the disbelief of those around them:

    a. Strongly agree

    b. Agree

    c. Disagree

    d. Strongly disagree

10. I believe the Holy Scriptures (the Bible) supports violence against women:

    a. Strongly agree

    b. Agree

    c. Disagree

    d. Strongly disagree

11. I consider sexual and physical violence against woman as a social justice issue.

    a. Most-likely

    b. Likely

    c. Somewhat likely

    d. Not likely

12. Are you willing to advocate for and speak on behalf of those who are under duress of sexual and physical violence?

    a. Most-likely

    b. Likely

    c. Somewhat likely

    d. Not likely

Pre-Survey Questionnaire for Leadership

1. Within the last year, how many times have you preached or heard a sermon addressing the issue of sexual and or physical violence against women:

    a. 1 – 2 times

    b. 3 – 5 times

    c. More than 5 times

    d. Not at all

2. How likely would you preach a sermon about sexual and physical abuses against women?

    a. Most-likely

    b. Likely

    c. Somewhat likely

    d. Not likely

3. How important would you rate the need for learning tools and resources to equip church leaders to be supportive of women that have been sexually and physically violated?

    a. Strongly agree

    b. Agree

    c. Disagree

    d. Strongly disagree

4. As a spiritual leader, do you perceive yourself to have influence on the congregation's awareness of the issue of sexual and physical abuse?

    a. Strongly agree

    b. Agree

    c. Disagree

    d. Strongly disagree

5. How significant is your role, as a church leader, to affirm women that have been traumatized by sexual and or physical violence?

    a. Strongly agree

    b. Agree

    c. Disagree

    d. Strongly disagree

6. How likely would you promote and lead discussions about the importance of addressing sexual and physical violence against women, from the pulpit, with other church leaders?

    a. Most-likely

    b. Likely

    c. Somewhat likely

    d. Not likely

7. How likely would you preach or teach those difficult scriptures about violence against women, from the perspective of the violated? (i.e. , Dinah, Tamar, Jephthah's Daughter, the Woman at the well, the Judges 19 Concubine, etc.)

    a. Most-likely

    b. Likely

    c. Somewhat likely

    d. Not likely

8. How likely would you attend training of how to dismantle the silence in the church, and how to affirm women that have been victimized?

    a. Most-likely

    b. Likely

    c. Somewhat likely

    d. Not likely

9. I am familiar with the sexual and physical abuse resources and agencies within the community.

    a. Strongly agree

    b. Agree

    c. Disagree

    d. Strongly disagree

10. Which would best describe how you have dealt with physical (domestic) abuse situations:

    a. Reported the incident to the police or another government agency.

    b. Recommended or provided couples counseling.

    c. Advised the victim to leave the volatile environment.

    d. I did not respond to the accusation.

    e. I have not had to deal with any domestic (physical) violence situations.

Weekly Survey

Sermon Title: _____

Sermonic Text: _____

Age _____

Gender _____

Numeric Identifier _____

1. Was the sermon topic/meaning clearly expressed?

    a. Totally reflects/is relevant (Excellent)

    b. Embraces most of the text (Good)

    c. Somewhat (Fair)

    d. Does not reflect/not relevant (Poor)

2. Did the sermon challenge your level of comfortability in a manner that is impactful and life-altering in respect to the issue?

    a. Totally reflects/is relevant (Excellent)

    b. Embraces most of the text (Good)

    c. Somewhat (Fair)

    d. Does not reflect/not relevant (Poor)

3. Did the sermon enhance or enlighten your understanding of the scripture text?

    a. Totally reflects/is relevant (Excellent)

    b. Embraces most of the text (Good)

    c. Somewhat (Fair)

    d. Does not reflect/not relevant (Poor)

4. Based on the sermon, did it encourage you to reengage the text through a different lens?

    a. Yes

    b. Somewhat

    c. No

5. Was the sermon relevant to the issues concerning the victimization of women today?

    a. Totally reflects is relevant (Excellent)

    b. Embraces most of the text (Good)

    c. Somewhat (Fair)

    d. Does not reflect / not relevant (Poor)

6. Was the sermon relative to the issue of sexual and phys-ical abuse?

   a. Totally reflects/is relevant (Excellent)

   b. Embraces most of the text (Good)

   c. Somewhat (Fair)

   d. Does not reflect/not relevant (Poor)

7. Did the sermon frustrate, anger, or disturb you?

   a. Totally reflects/is relevant (Excellent)

   b. Embraces most of the text (Good)

   c. Somewhat (Fair)

   d. Does not reflect/not relevant (Poor)

8. Did the sermon promote self-reflection?

   a. Totally reflects/ is relevant (Excellent)

   b. Embraces most of the text (Good)

   c. Somewhat (Fair)

   d. Does not reflect / not relevant (Poor)

9. How likely are you to share or reference this sermon with others?

    a. Most-likely

    b. Likely

    c. Somewhat likely

    d. Not likely

10. Is the sermon helpful in promoting personal awareness of sexual and physical abuses of women and the need to break the silence?

    a. Totally reflects/is relevant (Excellent)

    b. Embraces most of the text (Good)

    c. Somewhat (Fair)

    d. Does not reflect/not relevant (Poor)

Weekly Focus Group Survey

Sermon Title: _____

Sermonic Text: _____

Age _____

Gender _____

Numeric Identifier _____

1. Was the sermon topic clear?

    a. Totally reflects/is relevant (Excellent)

    b. Embraces most of the text (Good)

    c. Somewhat (Fair)

    d. Does not reflect / not relevant (Poor)

2. Was the sermon relative to the issue of sexual and physical abuse?

    a. Totally reflects/is relevant (Excellent)

    b. Embraces most of the text (Good)

    c. Somewhat (Fair)

    d. Does not reflect/not relevant (Poor)

3. What did you take away from this week's sermon?

    Comments:

4. Were you encouraged by the sermon?

    a. Totally reflects is relevant (Excellent)

    b. Embraces most of the text (Good)

    c. Somewhat (Fair)

    d. Does not reflect/not relevant (Poor)

5. Did the sermon frustrate, anger, or disturb you negatively?

    a. Totally reflects/is relevant (Excellent)

    b. Embraces most of the text (Good)

    c. Somewhat (Fair)

    d. Does not reflect/not relevant (Poor)

6. Did the sermon promote self-reflection?

    a. Totally reflects/is relevant (Excellent)

    b. Embraces most of the text (Good)

    c. Somewhat (Fair)

    d. Does not reflect/not relevant (Poor)

7. Did the sermon give you a sense of empowerment over the experience of abuse (minimizing the shame associated with abuse)?

    a. Totally reflects/is relevant (Excellent)

    b. Embraces most of the text (Good)

    c. Somewhat (Fair)

    d. Does not reflect/not relevant (Poor)

8. Would you share this sermon and related materials with others?

    a. Totally reflects/is relevant (Excellent)

    b. Embraces most of the text (Good)

    c. Somewhat (Fair)

    d. Does not reflect/not relevant (Poor)

9. How effective is the combination of the sermon and weekly reflective-group discussion?

    a. Totally reflects/is relevant (Excellent)

    b. Embraces most of the text (Good)

    c. Somewhat (Fair)

    d. Does not reflect/not relevant (Poor)

10. Are the group discussions about the sermon helpful in promoting personal healing?

    a. Totally reflects/is relevant (Excellent)

    b. Embraces most of the text (Good)

    c. Somewhat (Fair)

    d. Does not reflect/not relevant (Poor)

Post-Survey for Congregation

Sermon Title: _____

Sermonic Text: _____

Age _____

Gender _____

Numeric Identifier_____

1. Was the sermon topic clear?

    a. Totally reflects/is relevant (Excellent)

    b. Embraces most of the text (Good)

    c. Somewhat (Fair)

    d. Does not reflect/not relevant (Poor)

2. Was the sermon relative to the issue of sexual and physical abuse?

    a. Totally reflects is relevant (Excellent)

    b. Embraces most of the text (Good)

    c. Somewhat (Fair)

    d. Does not reflect/not relevant (Poor)

3. What did you take away from this week's sermon?

    Comments:

4. Were you encouraged by the sermon?

    a. Totally reflects/is relevant (Excellent)

    b. Embraces most of the text (Good)

    c. Somewhat (Fair)

    d. Does not reflect/not relevant (Poor)

5. Did the sermon frustrate, anger, or disturb you negatively?

    a. Totally reflects/is relevant (Excellent)

    b. Embraces most of the text (Good)

    c. Somewhat (Fair)

    d. Does not reflect/not relevant (Poor)

6. Did the sermon promote self-reflection?

    a. Totally reflects/is relevant (Excellent)

    b. Embraces most of the text (Good)

    c. Somewhat (Fair)

    d. Does not reflect/not relevant (Poor)

7. Did the sermon give you a sense of empowerment over the experience of abuse (minimizing the shame associated with abuse)?

    a. Totally reflects/is relevant (Excellent)

    b. Embraces most of the text (Good)

    c. Somewhat (Fair)

    d. Does not reflect/not relevant (Poor)

8. Would you share this sermon and related materials with others?

    a. Totally reflects/is relevant (Excellent)

    b. Embraces most of the text (Good)

    c. Somewhat (Fair)

    d. Does not reflect/not relevant (Poor)

9. How effective is the combination of the sermon and weekly reflective-group discussion?

    a. Totally reflects/is relevant (Excellent)

    b. Embraces most of the text (Good)

    c. Somewhat (Fair)

    d. Does not reflect/not relevant (Poor)

10. Are the group discussions about the sermon helpful in promoting personal healing?

    a. Totally reflects/is relevant (Excellent)

    b. Embraces most of the text (Good)

    c. Somewhat (Fair)

    d. Does not reflect/not relevant (Poor)

Post-Survey for Leadership

1. Within the last year, how many times have you preached or heard a sermon addressing the issue of sexual and or physical violence against women:

    a. 1 – 2 times

    b. 3 – 5 times

    c. More than 5 times

    d. Not at all

2. How likely would you preach a sermon about sexual and physical abuses against women?

    a. Most-likely

    b. Likely

    c. Somewhat likely

    d. Not likely

3. How important would you rate the need for learning tools and resources to equip church leaders to be supportive of women that have been sexually and physically violated?

    a. Strongly agree

    b. Agree

    c. Disagree

    d. Strongly disagree

4. As a spiritual leader, do you perceive yourself to have influence on the congregation's awareness of the issue of sexual and physical abuse?

    a. Strongly agree

    b. Agree

    c. Disagree

    d. Strongly disagree

5. How significant is your role, as a church leader, to affirm women that have been traumatized by sexual and or physical violence?

   a. Strongly agree

   b. Agree

   c. Disagree

   d. Strongly disagree

6. How likely would you promote and lead discussions about the importance of addressing sexual and physical violence against women, from the pulpit, with other church leaders?

   a. Most-likely

   b. Likely

   c. Somewhat likely

   d. Not likely

7. How likely would you preach or teach those difficult scriptures about violence against women, from the perspective of the vio-lated? (i.e. , Dinah, Tamar, Jephthah's Daughter, the Woman at the well, the Judges 19 Unnamed Concubine, etc.)

    a. Most-likely

    b. Likely

    c. Somewhat likely

    d. Not likely

8. How likely would you attend training of how to dismantle the silence in the church, and how to affirm women that have been victimized?

    a. Most-likely

    b. Likely

    c. Somewhat likely

    d. Not likely

9. I am familiar with the sexual and physical abuse resources and agencies within the community.

    a. Strongly agree

    b. Agree

    c. Disagree

    d. Strongly disagree

10. Which would best describe how you have dealt with physical (domestic) abuse situations:

    a. Reported the incident to the police or another government agency.

    b. Recommended or provided couples counseling.

    c. Advised the victim to leave the volatile environment.

    d. I did not respond to the accusation.

    e. I have not had to deal with any domestic (physical) violence situations.

Consent Forms

Transcriber

Consent Form to Participate in Research Study
(Please read the consent form in its entirety before signing)

You are being asked to participate, as **a recording transcriber,** in a research study that I, <u>Marcia R. Grayson</u>, am conducting as a Doctor of Ministry: Transformational Preaching candidate at the New Brunswick Theological Seminary under the advisement of my faculty advisor <u>Dr. Faye Banks Taylor</u> as part of my doctoral study entitled <u>"Using Transformational Preaching to Bring Awareness and Break the Silence in Congregations Regarding Sexual and Physical Abuse Against Women."</u> Your participation in this study is entirely voluntary. Please read the information below and ask questions about anything you do not understand before deciding whether or not to participate. Again, the decision to join, or not to join, is up to you. If you volunteer to be in this study, you may withdraw at any time without consequences of any kind. You may also refuse to answer any question you do not want to answer.

PURPOSE OF THE STUDY

This research project will answer the question, will the use of transformative sermons promote a change in the congregation's understanding of the importance of breaking the silence, within the church, and procure a community that affirms women in the congregation that have been detrimentally affected by such atrocities?

PROCEDURE

If you volunteer to participate in this study, you will be asked to do the following:

1. Attend the weekly worship services and participate in group discussions, and complete pre, post and weekly surveys, as well as maintain the anonymity of all focus group participants.
2. All information recorded and transcribed is not to be shared or discussed outside of the parameters of this research and with anyone that is not designated. Designees are the members of my Covenant Team, my faculty advisor, and the Doctor of Ministry Review Committee.
3. The information and collected data gained from this research study will be shared confidentially with my Covenant Team members, my faculty advisor, the Doctor of Ministry

Review Committee and may be used in my final dissertation project and publishing.

POTENTIAL BENEFITS

This study will give you an opportunity to share your views, opinions, and experiences. Your participation will inform the effects of preaching for sermon formulation and the effects of transformational preaching to bring awareness to congregations concerning the importance of the church addressing sexual and physical violence against woman. In addition, it will be used as an educational and instructional tool to heighten the awareness of preachers and pastors to address women who are hurting as a result of sexual and physical abuses, through the use of transformational preaching.

POTENTIAL RISKS

This project is not intended to provoke any physical, emotional or professional discomfort. There is no compensation for your participation or for any resulting desire to seek medical treatment of any kind.

CONFIDENTIALITY

Any information that is obtained, in connection with this study, will be used to write my dissertation. If you wish to participate in the study, please fill out the following form, and thank you for your participation.

Date_____

I, _____ give consent to <u>Marcia R. Grayson,</u> Doctoral Candidate at New Brunswick Theological Seminary, for my participation as the **recording transcriber,** in the research study tentatively entitled: <u>"Using Transformational Preaching to Bring Awareness and Break the Silence in Congregations Regarding Sexual and Physical Abuse Against Women."</u> It has been fully explained to me that the purpose of the study is as follows:

- I understand and agree how data will be collected.
- I understand that I may withdraw my consent and discontinue participation in this study at any time.
- I understand that by participating in this study I may help the researcher gain a better understanding of the theological issues inherent in their topic as they engage the academy, the church, and the community in their research endeavor.
- If I have further questions concerning the research study, I can feel free to contact candidate's Advisor **Dr. Faye Banks Taylor** at <u>ftaylor@nbts.edu</u> at any time.
- I understand the confidentiality of this project.
- I have received a copy of this consent form.
- I have read and understand the purpose of this study and voluntarily consent to participate.

Signature of Participant _____

Witness _____

General (Leadership and Focus Group)

<u>CONSENT FORM TO PARTICIPATE IN RESEARCH STUDY</u>
(Please read the consent form in its entirety before signing)

You are being asked to participate in a research study that I, <u>Marcia R. Grayson</u>, am conducting as a Doctor of Ministry in Transformational Preaching candidate at the New Brunswick Theological Seminary under the advisement of my faculty advisor <u>Dr. Faye Banks Taylor</u> as part of my doctoral study entitled <u>"Using Transformational Preaching to Bring Awareness</u> and Break the <u>Silence in Congregations Regarding Sexual and Physical Abuse of Women."</u> Your participation in this study is entirely voluntary. Please read the information below and ask questions about anything you do not understand before deciding whether to participate. Again, the decision to join, or not to join, is up to you. If you volunteer to be in this study, you may withdraw at any time without consequences of any kind. You may also refuse to answer any question you do not want to answer.

PURPOSE OF THE STUDY

This research project will answer the question, will the use of transformative sermons promote a change in the congregation's understanding of the importance of breaking the silence, within the church, and procure a community that affirms women in the congregation that have been detrimentally affected by such atrocities?

PROCEDURE

If you volunteer to participate in this study, you will be asked to do the following:

1. Attend the weekly worship services and participate in group discussions, and complete pre, post and weekly surveys, as well as maintain the anonymity of all focus group participants.
2. The information and collected data gained from this research study will be shared confidentially with my Covenant Team members, my faculty advisor, the Doctor of Ministry

Review Committee and may be used in my final dissertation project and publishing.

POTENTIAL BENEFITS

This study will give you an opportunity to share your views, opinions, and experiences. Your participation will inform the effects of preaching for: sermon formulation and the effects of transformational preaching to bring awareness to congregations concerning the importance of the church addressing sexual and physical violence against woman. In addition, it will be used as an educational and instructional tool to heighten the awareness of preachers and pastors to address women who are hurting as a result of sexual and physical abuses, through the use of transformational preaching.

POTENTIAL RISKS

This project is not intended to provoke any physical, emotional or professional discomfort. There is no compensation for your participation or for any resulting desire to seek medical treatment of any kind.

CONFIDENTIALITY

Any information that is obtained, in connection with this study, that can be identified with you will remain confidential and will be disclosed only with your permission or as required by law. Confidentiality will be maintained by using a three-digit numerical identifier instead of your name. I will keep tapes separated from the transcripts. Information obtained, in connection with this study, will be used to write my dissertation.

If you wish to participate in the study, please fill out the following form, and thank you for your participation.

Date_____

I, _____ give consent
to <u>Marcia R. Grayson,</u> Doctoral Candidate at New Brunswick
Theological Seminary, for my participation in the research study
tentatively entitled: <u>"Using Transformational Preaching to Bring</u>
<u>Awareness and Break the Silence in Congregations Regarding</u>
<u>Sexual and Physical Abuse Against Women."</u> It has been fully
explained to me that the purpose of the study is as follows:

- I understand and agree how data will be collected.
- I understand that I may withdraw my consent and discontinue participation in this study at any time.
- My identity and personal information will be kept confidential.
- I understand that by participating in this study I may help the researcher gain a better understanding of the theological issues inherent in their topic as they engage the academy, the church, and the community in their research endeavor.
- If I have further questions concerning the research study, I can feel free to contact candidate's Advisor Dr. Faye Banks Taylor at ftaylor@nbts.edu at any time.
- I have received a copy of this consent form.
- I have read and understand the purpose of this study and voluntarily consent to participate.

Signature of Participant _____

Witness _____

Scriptures and Sermons, Orders of Service

Sermon One: "The Time is Now."

Scripture: Isaiah 61:1-3

> The spirit of the Lord God is upon me, because the Lord has anointed me; he has sent me to bring good news to the oppressed, to bind up the brokenhearted, to proclaim liberty to the captives, and release to the prisoners; to proclaim the year of the Lord's favor, and the day of vengeance of our God; to comfort all who mourn; to provide for those who mourn in Zion—to give them a garland instead of ashes, the oil of gladness instead of mourning, the mantle of praise instead of a faint spirit. They will be called oaks of righteousness, the planting of the Lord, to display his glory.

Prayer

Isaiah 61:1-3 is the thematic scripture for my dissertation. We will explore other scriptures that connect to the proclamation of the thematic scripture. We will be exploring the scriptures that tell of the violations of Tamar, Dinah, and the Unnamed Concubine, they are examples of the "brokenhearted, oppressed, captives, and imprisoned" depicted in the Isaiah 61:1-3 passage. We will explore and preach those difficult scriptures that explicitly depict violence against women.

I want to share with you all a few vitally important statistics

1. Sexual and Physical Violence Statistics: Female victims of physical and sexual abuses.

   • African-American women
     o "An estimated 29. 1% of African American females are victimized by intimate partner violence in their life-time (rape, physical assault or stalking).
     o African American females experience intimate partner violence at a rate 35% higher than that of white females, and about 2. 5 times the rate of women of other races. However, they are less likely than white women to use social services, battered women's programs or go to the hospital because of domestic violence.
     o According to the National Violence Against Women Survey (NVAWS), African American women experi-ence higher rates of intimate partner homicide when compared to their White counterparts.
     o Statistics show that African American women typically comprise about 70% of black congregations. Religious convictions and a fear of shame or rejection from the church may contribute to their remaining in an abusive relationship."[85]

   • All women
     o Domestic Violence: A person is abused in the United States every 9 seconds (Bureau of Justice Statistics). [86]

o   Sexual Violence: 1 in 4 women and 1 out of 6 men are sexually abused in their lifetime (Department of Justice).[87]

o   "Globally, as many as 38% of murders of women are committed by an intimate partner, 200 million women have experienced female genital mutilation/cutting. 35% of women worldwide have experienced either physical and/or sexual intimate partner violence or non-partner sexual violence and Globally, 7% of women have been sexually assaulted by someone other than a partner."[88]

2.   Campus Rapes: Rape and Sexual Assault Among College-age Females, 1995-2013. "This statistical analysis compares the characteristics of rape and sexual assault victimization against females ages 18 to 24 who are enrolled and not enrolled in college. For both college students and nonstudents, the offender was known to the victim in about 80% of rape and sexual assault victimizations. Rape and sexual assault victimizations of students (80%) were more likely than nonstudent victimizations (67%) to go unreported to police. "[89] Dr. Leslie offers a statistical observation of sexual assaults. She states that "between 20-25% of women on college campuses experience rape and approximately 84% of those are acquaintance rapes."[90]

---

[87] The Center for Family Justice: Statistics

[88] The Center for Family Justice: Statistics

[89] Assault, South Eastern Center Against Sexual. South Eastern CASA. March 13, 2017. https://www.secasa. com.au/pages/feelings-after-sexual-assault/ (accessed 06 06, 2018).

[90] Leslie, Kristen J. "When Violence is No Stranger: Pastoral Care and Acquaintance Rape." *Journal of Religion and Abuse 3*, 2001: 77-78.

3. Pastoral survey: Out of 1,000 protestant pastors, a significant number do not consider sexual and domestic violence to be central to be preached. They believe the large central topics to be preached are "strong families, peaceful society, pursuing holiness, and social justice."[91] This is very interesting, because sexual and domestic violence is connected to each of these issues. My questions to you are

    *   Is the family strong if domestic violence is in the household?
    *   Is the society peaceful when women are being raped?
    *   In pursuing holiness, is that supposed to be without wholeness?
    *   Is not this issue of sexual and physical abuse, an injustice that effects the social thread of our society?

Eventually, as I have stated previously, we will explore Dinah, Tamar, the Unnamed Concubine.

As I began to explore these scriptures and the data of various research information, I've concluded that the main issue surrounding this issue is a systemic issue. The root of this issue goes back to the fact that we live in a patriarchal society. We live in a society that everything we have been taught to do has been passed down to us and impressed upon us by men. Our society is based on the mindset, thoughts, and opinions of men. As well as the stronghold that men have on women in seemingly every area of our lives. I notice that the patriarchal society is not only an issue of biblical times, but it is alive and present in the world today. Is not the Bible written been interpreted and written by all men? Have they not passed down their opinion of various things, such as, who

---

[91] Assault, South Eastern Center Against Sexual. *South Eastern* CASA. March 13, 2017. https://www.secasa. com.au/pages/feelings-after-sexual-assault/ (accessed 06 06, 2018).

we are as women, how we should be, how we should act, how we should act? Patriarchy is our society is not just a male thing, but it is engrained through white privilege.

I realize that women, African-American women especially, have a three-dimensional layer concerning the issue of discrimination. We're not only dealing with racism, but we are also dealing with sexism and classism. There was a point in time in America where there was racial inequality, I said there was a "point in time," –hello, in America. However, in that inequality, it was something that our African-American men forgot. They forgot that African-American women were standing by their side, were fighting with and for them, while we were all fighting for racial equality. Somewhere along the way, African American men also forgot that we are their women. I take that back, they didn't forget that we are their women, what they neglected to remember is that we are their partners, we were going through the same thing they were going through, and we, too, were hurting. The poisonous idea society was passing down that caused this division between African American men and women is that women are property. Did African American men forget that they too were once property – slaves of White men? When viewed as someone's property, one can do what one wants to do with their property; they can mistreat it, destroy it, abuse it, reprogram it, regulate, and silence their property. Even in biblical times, men made it plain that women were not equal. God forbid you were a widow without sons, you would be left out there to survive the best way you knew how. Women didn't even have equal rights to an inheritance that was left by the deceased. Somewhere along the line, women were declared to be property. We women were regarded as "less than".

Moving forward from biblical days, it took a very long time for any woman to acquire status. Both White and Black women struggled to have the right to vote, which was a feat in itself. However, women are still struggling to get equal pay for equal work, to have some of the same privileges of male counterparts in various fields, military, clerical and business. I have to make a confession. I have to confess that yes, we are the weaker sex genetically and physically; however, not mentally or educationally, not in ability, and not in integrity. Men were commanded to take care of their women. God gave Adam Eve in order for him to take care of and protect, but somewhere along the line, the patriarchal society began to stream down upon all men that women were not created equal, women are not to be regarded as equals, that women are property. There are some countries where women are to walk behind men and not beside them. There are even some cultures that believe that even the mother is subject to the son. For instance, riding in the car, the father and the young son sit in front and the mother is to take a back seat to her son, —there is something wrong there.

But there is good news. In this good news, the Word of God says, "the Spirit of the Lord God is upon me, because the Lord has anointed me, he has sent me to bring good news to the oppressed, to bind up the brokenhearted, to proclaim liberty to the captives, and release to the prisoners. I want to say that the time is now! In the book of Luke, Jesus goes into the synagogue and he opens the book and turns to this same writing, Isaiah 61, but there is something else that Jesus added, Jesus said "Today this scripture has been fulfilled. " Afterwards, sometime later, Jesus died and appeared unto the disciples when they were hiding behind closed and locked doors, he blew onto them the Holy Spirit and gave them the command to "Go ye therefore. " Jesus also had said unto them, that greater works than these that I have done, shall you all l do. That means that we are all in the appointed time of the year of the Lord, and it's time for the church to come together, it's time for the church to step up, it's time for church to make a difference, it's time for the church to jump into position! It's time for

166

us to get rid of our stinkin' thinkin'. It's time, today the scripture is not only fulfilled its mission to fulfill is now! It's time for us to realize that the women who are sitting in the church are equal in their stature, in their sacrifice, in their time, in their struggle and in their Christian journey.

Granted, we preachers are preaching in our churches, we are preaching to various situations and circumstances, yet we're not preaching to the hurt of our women. Women are sitting in the pews, silently screaming, "we are here, we have been hurt, we have been muzzled, we have been crushed, we have been abused, we have been left out, but we are here because we believe." We believe in God the Father, God the Son, God the Holy Spirit and we support our male congregants. But we are in a place to where we come, and we've been sitting quietly waiting for God to speak to our situation. We've been waiting for God to speak to our hurt. We've been waiting for God to remove the stigma of what has been regarded as disgraceful because of our foul experiences. We have had to be quiet about Uncle So-and-So messing with us, about Deacon Such-and-Such being home beating up his wife, and that the church knows that that father there has been touching on his child and didn't have any business touching them "there. " The Church knows that this husband is raping his wife. Many feels that since the couple is married, she doesn't have the right to say no or that he has the right to take "it," Not so! We have come to the time of talking, and that the time is now!

As women, all of our hurts and needs are not being preached to... yes, they're preaching to the fact that we all need a breakthrough, yes they're preaching to the fact that we need a financial blessing, yes they're preaching to the fact that someone wants a husband or wife, yes they're preaching to the fact that we have these basic every day needs, but they're missing the heart of the matter. The heart of the matter is the fact that women are hurting differently, and women are the majority of the makeup of our churches. The church takes our money for our tithes, our offerings, and time through the responsibilities delegated to us. Yet, it is are silent to our pain or tells us to just get over it. It has said to us "You better not say nothing; you better not embarrass this family." Or it has said, "Don't bring that foolishness in this church." Or they say "Hussy, you shouldn't have been so fresh." Or worse they say, "If your skirts were long enough you wouldn't entice the men to look at you." But yet, as a woman, I've been hurt, and I've been violated and I'm coming to my church because that's what I believe in and that's all I know.

In this Isaiah passage I found encouragement in the statement, "to bind up the broken-hearted," I discovered something very interesting about binding. Binding is the action of fastening or holding together. In my study, Dr. Raquel St. Clair made it so clear and plain that we as women see God – not from the perspective that we are tied to Jesus in His struggles, in Jesus' hurts, pains and suffering, but that Jesus is tied together with us in our suffering, in our struggle, in our strife, in our hurt and in our disappointment.[92] Jesus is not holding on to us in order for us to carry his cross, Jesus is sustaining us during our cross-bearing events. Jesus has already borne his cross and in the binding of Jesus to us solidifies Jesus' promise to never leave us or forsake us. Even in the mist of our struggle, in the binding of the Jesus who's heart was broken, Jesus who suffered, Jesus who died, Jesus who was forsaken, Jesus who rose, Jesus who is victorious is joining in with us and partnering with us so that we could be set free, so that we don't have to struggle in vain. Women and men who are abused, you are not alone.

God has not forsaken thee.

---

[92] St. Clair, Raquel. "Womanist Biblical Interpretation." *True to Our Native Land: An African American New Testament Commentary*, 2007: 54-62.

Some of the scriptures we are going to venture into will cause you to wonder and ask, "Where is God?" How many times in our lifetimes have we said "God, where are you, I don't see you, where are you, God? I'm hurting? Where are You, I can't feel Your presence?" And it seems as though this is all we hear … silence. But I'm here to encourage you, even when you can't see God moving, when you can't hear God talking and even when you can't feel God's presence, God is here. God is there. I'll tell you something else, I believe that there are times when we are so caught up in the situation, that the situation makes us deaf to the voice of God and null to the fact that God is actually present, hearing us and responding to our issue. Because we are so deeply, hurt, crushed and overtaken by loudly asking God, "**Where are you**?" when actually God is screaming in a small calming voice "I'm here, I'm here, I'm here, I promised you and I even wrote it down that I would never leave you or forsake you. I'm here my daughter, I'm here, I love you, I'm here, I sent Jesus for you, I'm here, I know it hurts but I am here, and I love you, I hear you and I feel you, I'm here. " God has come this year, 2019, to release us from ourselves. To release us from the deep-seated hurts that we have suppressed in the back of our minds. God is here for our wholeness, God created us whole, in God's image and likeness. "God has not given us the spirit of fear, but of love, power and a sound mind. "[93] During this journey we, as a congregation, shall come to a place to where we know more about physical and sexually violence against women, and we affirm those who have had those experiences. To affirm is to embrace those that have been abused, to let them know that the abuse was not their fault, they didn't do anything wrong, and they are not deserving of the abuse. To also show these women love and that as a church we are here for them. As Pastor Vanzant, Sr. has been

---

[93] 2 Timothy 1:7

preaching to us, that this church is a safe space congregation, to where no one is to be violated, especially in this church.

We are coming to a place that we will speak up and speak out against sexual and physical abuse against women. I love this church, I love this church, let me tell you why, there's something here that I have never really experienced. We have leaders and members that know what it means to march, to stand up for the rights of all people, and for the community. When there are fatal shootings, wrongful deaths, police brutality, whatever injustice that is affecting the community, this church will speak up, it will have a rally, or provide space for rallying, create space to have conversations, and if necessary, the people will march. Well church, it's time to march for this social justice issue of sexual and physical abuse against women. I remember Dr. Martin Luther King, Jr. said, "injustice anywhere is a threat to justice everywhere. " This issue of sexual and physical abuse is a threat to our well-being. Black, White, Hispanic, it doesn't matter what the skin color of the abused, we need to speak up for those who cannot speak up for themselves. We, the church, need to lend a voice to those who've been hushed until they are able to speak for themselves. We need to be strength to those who are weak until they are stronger. The time is now. God bless you.

https://youtu.be/LYAGrnEt6PI

Order of Service 2/6/19

Call to Worship and Invocation: Dr. Semaj Y. Vanzant, Sr.
Praise and Worship: Selection – "Lord You're Mighty"
Welcome and Statement of Purpose: Rev. Marcia Grayson
Selection: "Chasing After You"
Sermon: "The Time is Now." Isaiah 61:1-3

> "The spirit of the Lord God is upon me, because the Lord has anointed me; he has sent me to bring good news to the oppressed, to bind up the brokenhearted, to proclaim liberty to the captives, and release to the prisoners; to proclaim the year of the Lord's favor, and the day of vengeance of our God; to comfort all who mourn; to provide for those who mourn in Zion—to give them a garland instead of ashes, the oil of gladness instead of mourning, the mantle of praise instead of a faint spirit. They will be called oaks of righteousness, the planting of the Lord, to display his glory."

Altar call and Prayer
Offering: Deacons
Benediction

Sermon Two: "Can't You Hear Her?"

Scripture: 1 Samuel 13

1 Some time passed. David's son Absalom had a beautiful sister whose name was Tamar; and David's son Amnon fell in love with her. 2 Amnon was so tormented that he made himself ill because of his sister Tamar, for she was a virgin and it seemed impossible to Amnon to do anything to her. 3 But Amnon had a friend whose name was Jonadab, the son of David's brother Shimeah; and Jonadab was a very crafty man. 4 He said to him, "O son of the king, why are you so haggard morning after morning? Will you not tell me?" Amnon said to him, "I love Tamar, my brother Absalom's sister." 5 Jonadab said to him, "Lie down on your bed, and pretend to be ill; and when your father comes to see you, say to him, 'Let my sister Tamar come and give me something to eat, and prepare the food in my sight, so that I may see it and eat it from her hand. '" 6 So Amnon lay down, and pretended to be ill; and when the king came to see him, Amnon said to the king, "Please let my sister Tamar come and make a couple of cakes in my sight, so that I may eat from her hand. " 7 Then David sent home to Tamar, saying, "Go to your brother Amnon's house, and prepare food for him." 8 So Tamar went to her brother Amnon's house, where he was lying down. She took dough, kneaded it, made cakes in his sight, and baked the cakes. 9 Then she took the pan and set them out before him, but he refused to eat. Amnon said, "Send out everyone from me. " So, everyone went out from him. 10 Then Amnon said to Tamar, "Bring the food into the chamber, so that I may eat from your hand. " So, Tamar took the cakes she had made, and brought them into

the chamber to Amnon her brother. 11 But when she brought them near him to eat, he took hold of her, and said to her, "Come, lie with me, my sister." 12 She answered him, "No, my brother, do not force me; for such a thing is not done in Israel; do not do anything so vile! 13 As for me, where could I carry my shame? And as for you, you would be as one of the scoundrels in Israel. Now therefore, I beg you, speak to the king; for he will not withhold me from you." 14 But he would not listen to her; and being stronger than she, he forced her and lay with her. 15 Then Amnon was seized with a very great loathing for her; indeed, his loathing was even greater than the lust he had felt for her. Amnon said to her, "Get out!" 16 But she said to him, "No, my brother; for this wrong in sending me away is greater than the other that you did to me." But he would not listen to her. 17 He called the young man who served him and said, "Put this woman out of my presence, and bolt the door after her." 18 (Now she was wearing a long robe with sleeves; for this is how the virgin daughters of the king were clothed in earlier times.) So, his servant put her out, and bolted the door after her. 19 But Tamar put ashes on her head and tore the long robe that she was wearing; she put her hand on her head, and went away, crying aloud as she went. 20 Her brother Absalom said to her, "Has Amnon your brother been with you? Be quiet for now, my sister; he is your brother; do not take this to heart." So, Tamar remained, a desolate woman, in her brother Absalom's house. 21 When King David heard of all these things, he became very angry, but he would not punish his son Amnon, because he loved him, for he was his firstborn. 22 But Absalom spoke to Amnon neither good nor bad; for Absalom hated Amnon, because he had raped his sister Tamar.

Absalom Avenges the Violation of His Sister

²³ After two full years Absalom had sheepshearers at Baal-hazor, which is near Ephraim, and Absalom invited all the king's sons. ²⁴ Absalom came to the king, and said, "Your servant has sheepshearers; will the king and his servants please go with your servant?" ²⁵ But the king said to Absalom, "No, my son, let us not all go, or else we will be burdensome to you." He pressed him, but he would not go but gave him his blessing. ²⁶ Then Absalom said, "If not, please let my brother Amnon go with us." The king said to him, "Why should he go with you?" ²⁷ But Absalom pressed him until he let Amnon and all the king's sons go with him. Absalom made a feast like a king's feast. ²⁸ Then Absalom commanded his servants, "Watch when Amnon's heart is merry with wine, and when I say to you, 'Strike Amnon,' then kill him. Do not be afraid; have I not myself commanded you? Be courageous and valiant." ²⁹ So the servants of Absalom did to Amnon as Absalom had commanded. Then all the king's sons rose, and each mounted his mule and fled. ³⁰ While they were on the way, the report came to David that Absalom had killed all the king's sons, and not one of them was left. ³¹ The king rose, tore his garments, and lay on the ground; and all his servants who were standing by tore their garments. ³² But Jonadab, the son of David's brother Shimeah, said, "Let not my lord suppose that they have killed all the young men the king's sons; Amnon alone is dead. This has been determined by Absalom from the day Amnon raped his sister Tamar. ³³ Now therefore, do not let my lord the king take it to heart, as if all the king's sons were dead; for Amnon alone is dead. "

[34] But Absalom fled. When the young man who kept watch looked up, he saw many people coming from the Horonaim road by the side of the mountain. [35] Jonadab said to the king, "See, the king's sons have come; as your servant said, so it has come about." [36] As soon as he had finished speaking, the king's sons arrived, and raised their voices and wept; and the king and all his servants also wept very bitterly. [37] But Absalom fled, and went to Talmai son of Ammihud, king of Geshur. David mourned for his son day after day. 38 Absalom, having fled to Geshur, stayed there three years. [39] And the heart of the king went out, yearning for Absalom; for he was now consoled over the death of Amnon.

I have read this pericope in two voices: the traditional patriarchal view, and the view of Tamar's niece, who was named after her. Pamela Cooper-White, a feminist theologian, in her book, *The Cry of Tamar: Violence against Women and the Church's Response*, second edition, writes the story of Tamar and Ammon from the perspective of Tamar's niece. Tamar's niece has heard so much about her aunt from the retelling of the story by other women who gossiped about her aunt, who was disgraced and ran off to live with her brother's family. Therefore, causing Absalom and his family to flee as a result of him taking revenge on the behalf of his sister Tamar's honor. You know how folk do, they talk about things that have happened in secret, gossiping about events they speculate about and repeat them as true, as though they have experienced it for themselves or as if they were the fly on the wall.

As we take a look at Tamar, the rape of Tamar by her uncle, cousin, father, boyfriend, ex-husband, friend, …I mean her half-brother Ammon…, we enter into a word of violence and silence, betrayal and dismissal, a world back then that is happening even now. As the Word says, there's nothing new under the sun.

Unfortunately, the story stays the same, then and now. In this scripture the overtones of what has been dictated to us and as to what the outcome is to be, how the male dominant voice is the important and overshadowing voice of the scripture. Although Tamar has the ability to cry out and protest against her abuser, and reports her violence to her brother, her voice, her pain, her abuse, her embarrassment and her retribution is overshadowed by the male dominance of all that are around her. Her abuser dismisses her. Her brother hushes her. Her father never acknowledges her. Oddly, we never hear anything of her mother. There is plenty of testosterone flowing in this pericope. The dominant male voices take us to the point of view of all the men in the pericope. Their anger, their frustration, their revengeful plots, their hurt, their disappointment, and their despair. What about Tamar? What about her feelings, her pain, her disappointment, her violation, her anger, her bitterness? When does she speak? Well I say, let Tamar speak now.

Come go with me and my sanctified imagination from a womanist theologian's point of view. As we enter into my rendition of a hermeneutical technique called incarnational translation or as I affectionately coined the technique as a dramatic expression of the Word.

"My daddy kept complaining to momma about his son, my half-brother Anthony, being sick. Momma said, "he looked fine to me, after all his no-good hoodlum friends are over there with him all the time, can't be too sick." Daddy said, "whatever woman. Can you fix him something to eat and carry it over there?" "No Suh" momma said, "that's your boy, not mine. Besides where's his little hoochie entourage that's always over there since his momma left him that house and money?" Daddy said, "Woman I don't know, just send some food!" "Nope," she said. "Fine," daddy said, "he said he likes Tamar cooking better anyway, I'll send her over there."

"Marcia, I mean Svetlana, I mean Isabella, I mean Beth, oh my goodness, I mean Tamar!" "Yes daddy" I replied. "Go over there and fix your brother Anthony some dinner, he's not feeling well, and he likes your cooking, your momma being difficult." "Ok daddy I will." Although I'm only fourteen, I can burn! Granny taught me.

I don't mind going to fix Anthony some food, he treats me really special even though I'm just his half-sister. His whole sisters get mad because he's always so nice to me and buying me nice things. (PAUSE)

Little did we all know; Anthony had been plotting with that sneaky no good friend of his Peetie. I really don't like Peetie. Peetie told Anthony, "Get Tamar over here so you could have your way with her. Break Tamar in before anyone else has a chance to sample that sweet pure honey." Anthony agrees and puts this all into motion. (PAUSE)

Momma was nice enough to leave a few groceries on the table for me to take across the street to cook for Anthony. As I'm going out the door, my brother Odell pulls up. "Hey Odell!" "Hey Tamar," he says, "where you headin', baby girl?" "Daddy told me to go cook for Anthony because he's sick," I replied. He said, "you should've told him to order out!" We laughed as I replied, "next time I will! See you when I get back or are you just dropping in?" "Depends," he said, "did momma cook?" "Not yet", I said, "but she's got some stuff out." "Well", he said, "I'll prolly be here, you know momma loooove to talk while she's cooking and I loooove to eat!" (PAUSE)

I get to Anthony's door, just as I'm about to knock, Peetie comes out. He looks me up and down, licks his lips, and shouts back to Anthony, "Sweet lil honey, I mean Tamar is here. "Rolling my eyes at him as he leaves. I say to myself "I'm glad that jerk is gone."

(ROLE PLAY)

Tamar: Hey Anthony! Sorry you're not feeling so well. Ima fix you right on up. I'll fix enough so you'll have enough for leftovers for tomorrow.

Anthony: Hey Tamar, ok thanks, I'm going to go lay down while you cook. Not feeling too cool right now.

Tamar: Ok Anthony, I'll call you when it's done.

(Little did I know the devil was setting his trap).

Tamar: Anthony, your dinner is ready!

Anthony: Oh, ok Tamar, um can you bring it down to me, I'm not feeling all those stairs.

Tamar: Down, I wondered, why'd he go to the basement instead of to his room? Oh, I thought, the big screen TV. (Pause) Ok, coming! (so, I went and got a tray and carried his food down to him. As I got closer, he looked at me oddly, he had a sheet over his lap, and he looked naked under it.)

Tamar: Anthony why don't you have any clothes on?

Anthony: Oh, I'm sorry, I think it's my fever making me so hot.

Tamar: OK, well here's your food, I'm just going to leave it right here and go.

Anthony: Please Tamar, can you just put it on this little stand right here closer to me? I'm feeling a very weak. It smells good, I hope I can eat.

Tamar: OK. (So, I move closer to him to put the tray down, and all of a sudden, out of nowhere, he grabs me and pins me down, forcing my underclothes off!)

Tamar: NO ANTHONY STOP, PLEASE STOP DON'T DO THIS! PLEASE DADDY STOP! PLEASE UNCLE STOP! PLEASE COUSIN STOP! PLEASE DEACON STOP! PLEASE AUNTIE STOP HIM! PLEASE FRIEND STOP! PLEASE STOP BROTHER, STOOOOOP!

(I think to myself, O God, is it over? Then he has the nerve to get up and say)

Anthony: Get out of my sight you whore!

Tamar: Whore! You took IT from me! You stole my virginity, my life, my peace, my choice, my childhood, YOU STOLE ME! Now you're just going to throw me away, like it's all my fault!!!!

Anthony: Get Out!

Tamar: (As I walk slowly up the basement stairs with my clothes all ripped. this basement that has become the vault of my screams that will never be heard)

Tamar: They're never going to believe me. (Shaking my head and wringing my hands).

(End Role Play)

As I'm going home crying, bleeding and in pain, Odell sees me. He says, "Tamar, what's wrong? Did Anthony harm you?" "Yes!" I screamed. "Get in the car, you're going with me, he said. *I'll* be right back he continued. " But I followed him into the house, he was so mad, he didn't notice me. Odell begins to tell daddy what happened, but daddy's response was not what I was expecting, and neither was Odell's.

Daddy said, with tears and fear in his eyes, "Is Anthony ok, did you harm him?"

"Dad," Odell said, "are you serious right now? What about Tamar? You didn't even ask about her. She's crying, hurt, and bleeding, can't you hear her?"

Daddy says to him, "She's a woman now, what do you want me to do, what do you expect for me to say?" I just start to cry, in disbelief, and go get in Odell's car.

Odell comes out and gets in the car and says, "Don't worry baby girl, I'll take care of this."

So, my question is to you, the congregation, "Can you hear her?" Do you hear the women who have suffered abuse in our congregation, sitting quietly, hurting secretly, whose tears have been shut in the vault of their assault, screams that have been hushed, fear that has over taken them to the point to where their reality is, "they're never going to believe me. " Can you hear her, despite the fact that she's sitting with makeup on her face, sitting proper and prim? Can you hear her, as she is moving amongst the congregation as the usher, the deaconess, the minister, the preacher's wife or perhaps as the pastor? Can you hear her? Can you see her? Can you hear her silent tears? Can you hear her struggles? Are you really seeing or hearing her? Can you hear her shouting "stop!", as she replays it in her mind over and over again, knowing that her pleas and anguish have been stifled in the vault, which represents the place she was violated? What do we do? What do we do as a congregation? Do we speak up? Do we embrace? The answer is YES! And we must affirm them those women, affirm us women, affirm them and say, "It is not your fault, you did nothing wrong." "We love you; we are here for you. We care about you, please allow us love on you, Sis, I've been through the same thing." Or perhaps, "Sis, I don't know what happened, I can't even begin to imagine, but I'm here for you. I got you." Sis, I love you, I have your back and we're going to walk this journey together."

Lastly, I need you to know that what happened to you is not OK. God is not OK with this; God does not encourage violence. That is the work of the enemy. The trick of the enemy is to tell you that God said it's OK, but the Devil is a liar. We are here, in the person of God, to extend to you the love of God that is freely given. God wants you to know that God loves you best, and I love you too. If you don't believe it, come let me give you of hug of encouragement, if I may.

I pray that as we have taken a walk in the footsteps of today's Tamar, that you noticed the various names that were called in place of Tamar, that signify various cultures. This not an isolated issue. This is not a Black issue, this is not a White issue, this is not a Catholic or a Baptist issue, this is not just a Third-World country issue either, we are all affected by sexual assault and physical assault against women. However, the time is now for us to break the silence, to speak out against, and to speak up for women who have been sexually and physically violated.

Does not the word of God say, "If not my people who are called by my name, would humble themselves and pray, seek my face and turn from their wicked ways,"?[94] These wicked ways refer to the silence. It's time to break the silence and the wickedness of what

---

[94] 2 Chronicles 7:14

we have sat quietly by and allowed to happen. It's time to walk in the person of who God has created to be, as the people of God, to stand up for the rights of all people. "There's neither Greek or Jew, there is no longer slave or free, there is neither male and female; for all of you are new in Christ Jesus.[95]" It's time for us, the church, to respond to the hurts of all people. Amen.

https://youtu.be/NaiFJsBVFPk

---

[95] Galatians 3:28

Order of Service 2/13/14

Call to Worship and Invocation: Minister Kerwin Webb
First Scripture Reading: Samuel 13:1-22
Minister Cheron Whittaker

¹Some time passed. David's son Absalom had a beautiful sister whose name was Tamar; and David's son Amnon fell in love with her. ²Amnon was so tormented that he made himself ill because of his sister Tamar, for she was a virgin and it seemed impossible to Amnon to do anything to her. ³But Amnon had a friend whose name was Jonadab, the son of David's brother Shimeah; and Jonadab was a very crafty man. ⁴He said to him, "O son of the king, why are you so haggard morning after morning? Will you not tell me?" Amnon said to him, "I love Tamar, my brother Absalom's sister." ⁵Jonadab said to him, "Lie down on your bed, and pretend to be ill; and when your father comes to see you, say to him, 'Let my sister Tamar come and give me something to eat, and prepare the food in my sight, so that I may see it and eat it from her hand. '" ⁶So Amnon lay down, and pretended to be ill; and when the king came to see him, Amnon said to the king, "Please let my sister Tamar come and make a couple of cakes in my sight, so that I may eat from her hand. " ⁷Then David sent home to Tamar, saying, "Go to your brother Amnon's house, and prepare food for him." ⁸So Tamar went to her brother Amnon's house, where he was lying down. She took dough, kneaded it, made cakes in his sight, and baked the cakes. ⁹Then she took the pan and set them out before him, but he refused to eat. Amnon said, "Send out everyone from me. " So, everyone went out from him. ¹⁰Then Amnon said to Tamar, "Bring the food

into the chamber, so that I may eat from your hand. " So, Tamar took the cakes she had made, and brought them into the chamber to Amnon her brother. ¹¹But when she brought them near him to eat, he took hold of her, and said to her, "Come, lie with me, my sister." ¹²She answered him, "No, my brother, do not force me; for such a thing is not done in Israel; do not do anything so vile! ¹³As for me, where could I carry my shame? And as for you, you would be as one of the scoundrels in Israel. Now therefore, I beg you, speak to the king; for he will not withhold me from you." ¹⁴But he would not listen to her; and being stronger than she, he forced her and lay with her. ¹⁵Then Amnon was seized with a very great loathing for her; indeed, his loathing was even greater than the lust he had felt for her. Amnon said to her, "Get out!" ¹⁶But she said to him, "No, my brother; for this wrong in sending me away is greater than the other that you did to me. " But he would not listen to her. ¹⁷He called the young man who served him and said, "Put this woman out of my presence, and bolt the door after her." ¹⁸(Now she was wearing a long robe with sleeves; for this is how the virgin daughters of the king were clothed in earlier times.) So, his servant put her out, and bolted the door after her. ¹⁹But Tamar put ashes on her head and tore the long robe that she was wearing; she put her hand on her head, and went away, crying aloud as she went. ²⁰Her brother Absalom said to her, "Has Amnon your brother been with you? Be quiet for now, my sister; he is your brother; do not take this to heart." So, Tamar remained, a desolate woman, in her brother Absalom's house. ²¹When King David heard of all these things, he became very angry, but he would not punish his son Amnon, because he loved him, for he was his firstborn. ²²But Absalom spoke to Amnon neither good nor bad; for Absalom hated Amnon, because he had raped his sister Tamar.

Praise and Worship:"Just Want to Praise You."
Second Scripture Reading:2 Samuel 13:23-32
Minister Kerwin Webb

[23]After two full years Absalom had sheepshearers at Baal-hazor, which is near Ephraim, and Absalom invited all the king's sons. [24]Absalom came to the king, and said, "Your servant has sheepshearers; will the king and his servants please go with your servant?" [25]But the king said to Absalom, "No, my son, let us not all go, or else we will be burdensome to you." He pressed him, but he would not go but gave him his blessing. [26]Then Absalom said, "If not, please let my brother Amnon go with us." The king said to him, "Why should he go with you?" [27]But Absalom pressed him until he let Amnon and all the king's sons go with him. Absalom made a feast like a king's feast. [28]Then Absalom commanded his servants, "Watch when Amnon's heart is merry with wine, and when I say to you, 'Strike Amnon,' then kill him. Do not be afraid; have I not myself commanded you? Be courageous and valiant." [29]So the servants of Absalom did to Amnon as Absalom had commanded. Then all the king's sons rose, and each mounted his mule and fled. [30]While they were on the way, the report came to David that Absalom had killed all the king's sons, and not one of them was left. [31]The king rose, tore his garments, and lay on the ground; and all his servants who were standing by tore their garments. [32]But Jonadab, the son of David's brother Shimeah, said, "Let not my lord suppose that they have killed all the young men the king's sons; Amnon alone

is dead. This has been determined by Absalom from the day Amnon raped his sister Tamar.

Welcome and Statement of Purpose: Rev. Marcia Grayson
Third Scripture Reading: 2 Samuel 13:33-39
Deacon Mary Scott

[33]Now therefore, do not let my lord the king takes it to heart, as if all the king's sons were dead; for Amnon alone is dead. " [34]But Absalom fled. When the young man who kept watch looked up, he saw many people coming from the Horonaim road by the side of the mountain. [35]Jonadab said to the king, "See, the king's sons have come; as your servant said, so it has come about." [36]As soon as he had finished speaking, the king's sons arrived, and raised their voices and wept; and the king and all his servants also wept very bitterly. [37]But Absalom fled, and went to Talmai son of Ammihud, king of Geshur. David mourned for his son day after day. [38]Absalom, having fled to Geshur, stayed there three years. [39]And the heart of the king went out, yearning for Absalom; for he was now consoled over the death of Amnon.

Selection: "Lord You Are Good"
Sermon: "Can't You Hear Her?" 2 Samuel 13
Altar call and Prayer
Offering: Deacons
Benediction

Sermon Three: "The Absence of the Presence of God. "

Scripture: Judges 19:22-26

> "²²While they were enjoying themselves, the men of the city, a perverse lot, surrounded the house, and started pounding on the door. They said to the old man, the master of the house, "Bring out the man who came into your house, so that we may have intercourse with him." ²³ And the man, the master of the house, went out to them and said to them, "No, my brothers, do not act so wickedly. Since this man is my guest, do not do this vile thing. ²⁴ Here are my virgin daughter and his concubine; let me bring them out now. Ravish them and do whatever you want to them; but against this man do not do such a vile thing." ²⁵ But the men would not listen to him. So the man seized his concubine, and put her out to them. They wantonly raped her, and abused her all through the night until the morning. And as the dawn began to break, they let her go. ²⁶ As morning appeared, the woman came and fell down at the door of the man's house where her master was, until it was light."

Judges 19:1 begins with "In those days when there was no King in Israel."

There was a book written by Bill Wiese called *23 Minutes in Hell: One Man's Story About What He Saw, Heard, and Felt in that Place of Torment.* He speaks of his experience of being in Hell, not being tormented himself, but the feel, the darkness, the stench, the demons and the terrorizing screams of the hell experience. I believe he makes mention to the fact that with all of that going on, the worst part of hell was the absence of God's presence.

There are times in our lives when we may have the experience of missing the feeling of God in our lives. I know I do when I miss prayer many days in a row and when I don't read or hear a scripture or when I don't listen to my Gospel. Although this is a totally different type of missing God's presence, if you've been where I have in this description, then you know what it feels like to miss the interaction with God and the feeling of God's presence. Judges 19 begins with "In those days when there was no king in Israel." Chapter 21:25, it gives the concluding phrase to this statement, indicating the consequence of that statement; which is "every man did that which was right in his own eyes." This portion of the scripture helps us to understand that there was no moral compass in the heart of humanity that pointed towards God. Therefore, there was a lot of mess going on there. The same mess and corruption that is happening now because of the lack of the presence of God in the hearts of humankind. I would imagine that the darkness, stench, and demonic presence that Wiese experienced in hell, is the same darkness, demonic presence and stench that exist in the hearts of those who do not know God and do not have a *true* relationship with God.

I'm emphasizing *true* relationship because of the recent discoveries and uncovering's of those that have been placed in positions of trust and high respect, as religious leaders who are responsible for the spiritual well-being and growth of their congregants. However, there were approximately 188 names of Catholic priests and deacons who are accused of sexual abuse of minors dating back to 1940.[96] Additionally, the Pope has recently acknowledged the sexual abuse of nuns by priests and bishops as well to the fact that some nuns have given birth to children of priests, and others

---

[96] Heyboer, Kelly and Ted Sherman. "NJ.com True Jersey." *nj.com.* February 13, 2019. http://www.nj.com (accessed February 26, 2019).

have terminated pregnancies as a result of these sexual violations.[97] The Southern Baptist Convention is also contending with 250 of its leaders sexually abusing more than 700 congregants over the last 20 years. Sadly, a pastor in Brooklyn, NY, has recently been exposed for repeatedly sexually abusing his teenage daughter multiple years.[98] These individuals that are facing allegations of sexual assault are men in esteem leadership positions in various congregations, denominations, and locations. Each of these men is regarded as a man of God: a priest, a pastor, a member of the clergy, and are all held in high esteem in the eyes of their congregants, other clergy persons and within their communities. I'd like to suggest that the hearts of these individuals are suffering from the absence of the *real* presence of God. Just like the Levite in Judges 19.

This Levite, man of God is held in such high esteem by the man of the house, who persuaded the Levite and his concubine to stay with them for the night. He is held in such high esteem that the man of the house, who is the father of two virgin daughters, offers his daughters and the Levite's concubine to these ravenous men to be gang-raped for the sake of sparing the man of God. I have a problem with that.

Was there no other way to control these out-of-control hellish men? Did this situation actually call for a sacrifice? Did the sacrifice have to require the violation of two virgin women and the wife/concubine of the Levite? How does one justify this sacrifice, the sanctity of women? How does one disregard the choice of women? How does one validate the sexual exploitation of women? Even more importantly, how does one voluntarily defile the sanctity of women and girls?

---

[97] Hopkins, Anna. "Fox News." foxnews.com. January 13, 2019. http://www.foxnews.com (accessed February 26, 2019).

[98] Hopkins, Anna. "Fox News." foxnews.com. January 13, 2019. http://www.foxnews.com (accessed February 26, 2019).

Well let me tell you why, it's the systemic evil of patriarchy. Dr. Traci West defines patriarchy as a "systematic devaluation of the worth and value of women."[99] In other words, patriarchy creates a gender imbalance and supremacy. It promotes and elevates the importance of men over women while devaluing the humanness of women, by lowering women to the place of property. In the beginning when God created men and women in God's own likeness, God created men and women equal. Although God instructed men to be the head of women, and women to be the help-mate to men, nowhere in the Bible does it mention that God suffers from a dissociative identity disorder. If God created men and women in the image of God, then God does not see one as less or as property. Therefore, why do some men? Men who are predators find it easier to deny the presence of God in women, denying the image of God as a reflection of themselves.[100] It is unfortunate that this is the patriarchal society of which we live. Today, in some societies, women are still equated as property or less than, and are under the subjection of the brutality of sexual and physical assaults and mutilation because they are women. The same holds true for these women in Judges 19.

These women have been offered up and sacrificed by the very men they love, respect, and trust to protect and love them in return. Instead, they are offered up without the ability to have a choice in the matter concerning their own bodies. It appears that this same issue of telling women what they are to do with their bodies is still alive and well today. There are movements of Pro-life verses Pro-Choice. Pro-lifers believe the government (a patriarchal system) should enforce preservation of all human life. This is something I

---

[99] West, Traci C. Wounds of the Spirit: Black Women, Violence, and Resistance Ethics. New York and London: New York University Press, 1999.

[100] Coleman, Monica A. Making a Way Out of No Way: A Womanist Theology. Minneapolis : Fortress Press, 2008.

find very interesting. The government condones taking the life of another in the case of the death penalty, the government is condoning the unsubstantiated death of black people, particularly, the young black males. The government is also condoning the actions of those in high political status to sexually violate women without punishment or repercussion. Why? I dare say because of the two systemic evils that run deeply in the soul of America, White supremacy/privilege and patriarchy.

I begin to wonder what the thoughts of these women were while they were being discussed as the alternative to surrendering the man of God to these hoodlums. I wondered if they were okay with the offering of their purity, their souls, their sanctity and their choice. I wondered, "Did they plead with the father and the Levite not to be thrown out to those mean-spirited men?" I wonder how they finally arrived at the conclusion to send the unnamed concubine out alone to be raped all night by several men. All of these things in this pericope disturb me deeply. Reviewing the life of this woman, the unnamed concubine, and how she endured so much. She was in an abusive relationship with the Levite. Judges 1 alludes to the fact that she was abused by her husband the Levite, and fled home to her father, only to be sent back with the Levite when he came to retrieve her. I found it very peculiar that the mother is never mentioned and does not seem to play a role in the prevention of or the allowing of the daughter's return to the Levite. It made me wonder if there was generational curse of abuse and if abuse was an aggravating factor in the sending back of the unnamed concubine. Was the father abusing his wife also, therefore justifying sending back his daughter to an abusive spouse? Was the mother silent because her voice had been nullified because of the abusive behavior of the father towards her? Why had the mother been silenced and nonexistent in this pericope?

After the reuniting of the unnamed concubine and the Levite, she, the unnamed concubine, is forced to be sacrificed for his sake. She's savagely raped and then left on the bottom of the porch for dead. But she persevered and made it to the door, only to be stepped over by the Levite on his way home without her. As if that was not enough, this Levite, this husband takes her and throws her on the back of the mule to be toted home. Not cared for, no love, and no gratitude for her taking his place in the brutal rape that was meant for him. Too often, women are sacrificed for men. Women receive the anger, bitterness, and violence from men when men have had a bad day, have been ridiculed or belittled by other men or their bosses, and when men feel the pressures of life are too great for them to handle. Women are also victimized for the sake of the family. Women are silenced due to the viciousness of men, and most times their stories are never told. The unnamed concubine is silenced, dying without ever being able to tell her story. The severe, harsh and exasperating treatment of this woman is despicable. We have women in our communities, our churches, and probably our families that are silently suffering and trying to recover from last night's beating and violation. Like those three woman in this pericope, they have no one to speak up on their behalf, no one to say, "Stop the violence," no one to lend guidance as to where they can receive help and how to escape their situation. Church, we have to speak up, we have to let those victimized women who are sitting silently know that we care, we are here, that we want to help, that there is no reason to be ashamed, and it's not their fault. The scripture reads in Judges 21:25, "In those days there was no king in Israel; all the people did what was right in their own eyes," however, God is still there. We don't hear of God in this pericope, or in the dark places of the concubine's experience. She probably wondered, "God, where are you?" I want us all to know, that in the dark places in our lives, the ugly experiences of our lives, our God is always present. Even in the presence of evil, God will sustain us through dark and harsh times. Don't give up on God, God has us even as we go through difficulties and the harshness of life. Have confidence and have faith. The word of God says, "vengeance is mine saith the Lord, and I will repay."[101] It's in these difficult times that God promises to never leave us nor forsake us. God has not and is not punishing the victimized. In situations like this it is very difficult to see, feel, hear and even believe in God, but believe and trust God's promise to never leave or disown us. Be encouraged, even in the absence of the presence of God in the hearts of abusers, God is always present with us. Always remember, we are never alone.

https://youtu.be/eIv_Edez45E

---

[101] Deuteronomy 32:35 (New International Version).

Order of Service 2/27/19

Call to Worship and Invocation: Mrs. Mazie Wynn
Praise and Worship: "He's Able."
Welcome and Statement of Purpose: Rev. Marcia Grayson (Announce we will have last service on March 6, 2019 at 6 p.m. sharp. Then will have Lent Service but the focus group will convene downstairs and be back up in time to receive ashes.
Scripture Reading: Judges 19:21-26 NRSV

> [22]While they were enjoying themselves, the men of the city, a perverse lot, surrounded the house, and started pounding on the door. They said to the old man, the master of the house, "Bring out the man who came into your house, so that we may have intercourse with him." [23] And the man, the master of the house, went out to them and said to them, "No, my brothers, do not act so wickedly. Since this man is my guest, do not do this vile thing. [24] Here are my virgin daughter and his concubine; let me bring them out now. Ravish them and do whatever you want to them; but against this man do not do such a vile thing." [25] But the men would not listen to him. So, the man seized his concubine, and put her out to them. They wantonly raped her and abused her all through the night until the morning. And as the dawn began to break, they let her go. [26] As morning appeared, the woman came and fell down at the door of the man's house where her master was, until it was light."

Selection: "I Love You Jesus."
Sermon: "The Absence of the Presence of God" Judges 19:22-26
Altar call and Prayer
Offering: Deacons
Benediction

Sermon Four: "What's Love Got to Do with It?"

Scripture: Genesis 34

Now Dinah the daughter of Leah, whom she had borne to Jacob, went out to visit the women of the region. * When Shechem son of Hamor the Hivite, prince of the region, saw her, he seized her and lay with her by force. [3] And his soul was drawn to Dinah daughter of Jacob; he loved the girl and spoke tenderly to her. [4] So Shechem spoke to his father Hamor, saying, "Get me this girl to be my wife. " [5] Now Jacob heard that Shechem had defiled his daughter Dinah; but his sons were with his cattle in the field, so Jacob held his peace until they came. [6] And Hamor the father of Shechem went out to Jacob to speak with him, [7] just as the sons of Jacob came in from the field. When they heard of it, the men were indignant and very angry, because he had committed an outrage in Israel by lying with Jacob's daughter, for such a thing ought not to be done. [8] But Hamor spoke with them, saying, "The heart of my son Shechem longs for your daughter; please give her to him in marriage. [9] Make marriages with us; give your daughters to us, and take our daughters for yourselves. [10] You shall live with us; and the land shall be open to you; live and trade in it, and get property in it." [11] Shechem also said to her father and to her brothers, "Let me find favor with you, and whatever you say to me I will give. [12] Put the marriage present and gift as high as you like, and I will give whatever you ask me; only give me the girl to be my wife. "[13] The sons of Jacob answered Shechem and his father Hamor deceitfully, because he had defiled their sister Dinah. [14] They said to them, "We cannot do this thing, to give our sister to one who is uncircumcised, for that would be a disgrace to us. ^{15} Only on this condition will we consent to you: that you will become as we are and every male among you be circumcised. ^{16} Then we will give our daughters to you, and we will take your daughters for ourselves, and we will live among you and become one people. ^{17} But if you will not listen to us and be circumcised, then we will take our daughter and be gone. "^{18} Their words pleased Hamor and Hamor's son Shechem. ^{19} And the young man did not delay to do the thing, because he was delighted with Jacob's daughter. Now he was the most honored of all his family. ^{20} So Hamor and his son Shechem came to the gate of their city and spoke to the men of their city, saying, ^{21} "These people are friendly with us; let them live in the land and trade in it, for the land is large enough for them; let us take their daughters in marriage, and let us give them our daughters. ^{22} Only on this condition will they agree to live among us, to become one people: that every male among us be circumcised as they are circumcised. ^{23} Will not their livestock, their property, and all their animals be ours? Only let us agree with them, and they will live among us." ^{24} And all who went out of the city gate heeded Hamor and his son Shechem; and every male was circumcised, all who went out of the gate of his city. ^{25} On the third day, when they were still in pain, two of the sons of Jacob, Simeon and Levi, Dinah's brothers, took their swords and came against the city unawares, and killed all the males. ^{26} They killed Hamor and his son Shechem with the sword, and took Dinah out of Shechem's house, and went away. ^{27} And the other sons of Jacob came upon the slain, and plundered the city, because their sister had been defiled. ^{28} They took their flocks and their herds, their donkeys, and whatever was in the city and in the field. ^{29} All their wealth, all their little ones and their wives, all that was in the houses, they captured and made their prey. [30] Then Jacob said to Simeon and Levi, "You have brought trouble on me by making me odious to the inhabitants of the land, the Canaanites and the Perizzites; my numbers are few, and if they gather themselves against me and attack me, I shall be destroyed, both I and my household. " [31] But they said, "Should our sister be treated like a whore?"

As I looked over and over again at this pericope I perceived several violations against Dinah by men who seemingly love her. There are several variations of manipulation, coercion, and sexism that accompany the rape of Dinah. The first man to I noticed is Shechem, the privileged rapist, Hamon and Jacob, the deal making fathers for the sake of each of their family's name, and lastly, the angry and vengeful brothers (particularly Levi and Simeon) of Dinah. As usual in this patriarchal, sexist, and privileged society, these men did not consult with Dinah, take into consideration how she may be feeling, what her thoughts were, her emotional state of being or if she even wanted to be betrothed to Shechem. I mentioned the question of betrothal because after Dinah has been raped by Shechem and agreement is reached for Shechem to be allowed to marry Dinah. During this betrothal period, Dinah is forced to live under the same roof of her abuser. Hmmm. Unfortunately, there are many women who have had this cruel psychological and emotional experience. Women have had to grow up in the house with their abuser without being allowed to express their fear or to let anyone know what was happening to them because of the paralyzing effect of fear. Women have been raped by their fathers, brothers, cousins, uncles and close friends of the family and have been threatened into secrecy.

Fear is a very crippling emotion. I looked up the word fear and came across this very comprehensive definition from Bing:

> Fear is a feeling induced by perceived danger or threat that occurs in certain types of organisms, which causes a change in metabolic and organ functions and ultimately a change in behavior, such as fleeing, hiding, or freezing from perceived traumatic events. Fear in human beings may occur in response to a certain stimulus occurring in the present, or in anticipation or expectation of a future threat perceived as a risk to body or life. The fear response arises from the perception of danger leading to confrontation with or escape from/avoiding the threat, which in extreme cases of fear can be a freeze response or paralysis.[102]

If you have ever experienced fear in this magnitude, you will never understand the silencing and debilitating effect fear has on those that have been victimized. Believe me when I tell you, it is an experience that I would not wish on my worst enemy. Often, many find themselves in the seat of judgement when looking from the outside-in of an abusive situation. I'm explaining this because, as a congregation, we must be conscious and aware to not be judgmental, particularly when it comes to victims of abuse.

Let us continue. As the first abuser of Dinah in this pericope, it struck me odd and it annoyed me that after Shechem had raped Dinah he fell in love her. So much so that he went to his father demanding him to get her to be his wife. After such a violent act of raping her against her will, he now has the audacity to demand his father to go and get her to be his wife. It reminds me of the song Tina Turner sang and subsequently the name the movie that told of her story called, "What's Love Got to Do with It?" This

---

[102] Bing.com

movie tells of the abuse that Tina Turner suffered at the hands of her husband Ike Turner. Like the majority of abusive relationships, the abuser usually says something to the effect of "I love you baby, I don't' know why I did that." Why do you make me put my hands on you knowing how much I love you girl?" I get so crazy sometimes because I love you so much." Or this phrase, "Love you baby, I promise I won't do it again." Abusers say what makes them feel better and will help them justify the violent act they've committed. Unfortunately, we as women believe these lines and decide to stay with them, forgive them, keep loving them, and eventually, we too begin to believe they love us as we become complacent in the abusive relationship.

I could only imagine if Dinah was living in this century, she would probably inquire of Shechem and say, "What's love got to do with it, what's love but a second-hand emotion?" "You took it, got whipped, and *now* you want to "put a ring on it?" I would dare say, that because of his privilege and his father's position, he feels entitled to demand her to be his wife. Shechem does not even acknowledge that he has done an abominable offense and that he is wrong. Selfishly, he asks for her to be his wife, and his father agrees to secure this woman, that he raped, for his wife. This too, is problematic.

We often see in today's society how affluent people use their political and social influences, their Whiteness and money to buy themselves and their children out of trouble. Not only is Hamor concerned about covering up his son's atrocity, but also, he is concerned for his region. He needs to quickly make amends for the offense that was done against Jacob, Dinah's father, but not to Dinah, the one who is the victim. As these two fathers come together to try to come to a reasonable agreement to keep the peace in the land, neither of them actually attends to the needs, desires or pain of Dinah. Fathers! What are they thinking? Too often in our society and culture we find mothers and fathers silencing their daughters about sexual abuse by a relative for the sake of the family name. "Hush chil', don't you embarrass this family." "Stop telling those lies!" "If you say one word, you'll be on the street, I swear, I'll put you out!" Children and women should not be responsible for upholding the family name at the cost of sacrificing their own lives, purity, and sanity.

I have to admit; I admire the brothers just a little. Although these brothers, devised a scheme to avenge the rape of their sister and didn't ask or find out how she felt about it, they had enough sense to be offended by the offer of Hamor and Shechem to unite the two families. Truth be told, I think they may have been annoyed that their father had not taken any action against Hamor and Shechem before they arrived home.

Dinah's brothers had devised and executed a very evil and vile plan. However, after the plan was carried out, they did ask Jacob an important question, "Should our sister be treated like a whore?" This is the one time in this scripture that the integrity and character of Dinah is verbally considered. This is not something that Jacob ever seemed to have taken into consideration even during his initial reaction of Dinah being raped. However, Jacob's concern turns from Dinah to the possible disgrace on the family. Again, Jacob is putting himself, his honor and the appearance of "for the sake of the family," before his daughter Dinah. Yes, the brothers were wrong for violating the sanctity of circumcision, using this God instituted ritual to weaken the enemy, and for slaughtering all the men. This scheme to wipe out an entire city of men and steal all the valuables out of the city, leaving the women of the city alive but without a covering and provision. Their one sister was violated, and they violated an entire city of women. One act of violence does not negate the violence done to others. Of course, they did not see the fact that they too have violated and caused disparity for a city of women. I am not minimizing what happened Dinah at all. Unfortunately, in this biblical patriarchal and sexist society (even today), the actions of men dictate and cause a negative impact on women.

Laws are made and passed today on behalf of women, without allowing women to maintain their individual voices and choices. Am I Pro-Life? Yes, I am. Am I Pro-Choice? Yes, I am. I understand that choice belongs to the individual woman and her voice should never be taken away. The decision of Pro-Life or Pro-Choice, effects so many decisions, rights, and privileges on a spectrum that is much greater than the right to have an abortion or the right to stop abortion. It is akin to the brothers of Dinah decision to manipulate the law of God (circumcision), to where the effect is beyond one person. The repercussions of those issues threaten the welfare of women as well as women's right to make informed decisions, to be taken seriously as equals, to be seen as women in authority and leadership. I'm sure the movement meant well, but I do not believe they understood the long-standing and adverse impact that it would have on the voice, credibility, equality, and integrity of all women.

So, I ask you, "what does love got to do with it?" Well, I'm glad you asked. Love has everything to do with it and it's not "a second-hand emotion." "Love is patient; love is kind; love is not envious or boastful or arrogant or rude. It does not insist on its own way; it is not irritable or resentful; 6 it does not rejoice in wrongdoing but rejoices in the truth. It bears all things, believes all things, hopes all things, endures all things. Love never ends."[103] Love is not abusive. Love is not accusatory. Love is not judgmental. Love is affirming. Love extends to all, "For God so love the world that he gave his only Son, so that everyone who believes in him

---

[103] 1 Corinthians 13:4-8.

may not perish but may have eternal life. "[104] We, the church, are the extension of God and we must show love in all that we do. Showing love includes standing up for those who cannot stand up for themselves, showing love to those that have never experienced the love of God, giving love to those who have experienced abuse disguised as love. Love is the difference. "What's love got to do with it?" Everything.

We are "under an open heaven," God's glory shall be revealed. [105] As we unite this last sermon in this dissertation series, to our initial sermonic title, text "The time is Now," and Isaiah 61:1-3: "The spirit of the Lord God is upon me, because the Lord has anointed me; he has sent me to bring good news to the oppressed, to bind up the brokenhearted, to proclaim liberty to the captives, and release to the prisoners; to proclaim the year of the Lord's favor, and the day of vengeance of our God; to comfort all who mourn; to provide for those who mourn in Zion— to give them a garland instead of ashes, the oil of gladness instead of mourning, the mantle of praise instead of a faint spirit." That we, the women, the congregation, "shall stand be called oaks of righteousness, the planting of the Lord, to display his glory!" We are the people of God, we are the church of God, we are commanded to stand up for those who cannot stand up for themselves! We are the church that needs to extend the love of God! We are the church that cannot be judgmental! We are the ones that need to embrace those that do not know what it means to be genuinely embraced! This *is* acceptable year of the Lord! This is the year, 2019, the time is now for the church to stand, the time is now for the Church! The time is now. We can no longer be silent, we can no longer be idle, we can no longer turn a deaf ear (turning my back to the congregation). We must embrace those who have

---

[104]John 3:16

[105]Curtis, Miranda. "Open Heaven." Open Heaven: The Miranda Experience Live. Columbia / Fair Trade Services, 2018.

been victimized, we must love them; love is not a second-hand emotion, love is the gift that comes from God. "God so loved the world that he gave his only begotten Son,"[106] not that one, not that some, not that a few and not that even the one hundred forty-four thousand, but so that ALL may be saved.

https://youtu.be/1f6hsS6oFys

---

[106] John 3:16.

Order of Service 3/06/19

Call to Worship and Invocation:Deacon Damita Jo Warren
First Scripture Reading:Genesis 34:1-17
(Deaconess Martha Belcher)

[1]Now Dinah the daughter of Leah, whom she had borne to Jacob, went out to visit the women of the region. [2] When Shechem son of Hamor the Hivite, prince of the region, saw her, he seized her and lay with her by force. [3] And his soul was drawn to Dinah daughter of Jacob; he loved the girl, and spoke tenderly to her. [4] So Shechem spoke to his father Hamor, saying, "Get me this girl to be my wife. "[5] Now Jacob heard that Shechem had defiled his daughter Dinah; but his sons were with his cattle in the field, so Jacob held his peace until they came. [6] And Hamor the father of Shechem went out to Jacob to speak with him, [7] just as the sons of Jacob came in from the field. When they heard of it, the men were indignant and very angry, because he had committed an outrage in Israel by lying with Jacob's daughter, for such a thing ought not to be done. [8] But Hamor spoke with them, saying, "The heart of my son Shechem longs for your daughter; please give her to him in marriage. [9] Make marriages with us; give your daughters to us, and take our daughters for yourselves. [10] You shall live with us; and the land shall be open to you; live and trade in it, and get property in it." [11] Shechem also said to her father and to her brothers, "Let me find favor with you, and whatever you say to me I will give. [12] Put the marriage present and gift as high as you like, and I will give whatever you ask me; only give me the girl to be my wife. "[13] The sons of Jacob answered Shechem and his father Hamor deceitfully, because he had

defiled their sister Dinah. [14] They said to them, "We cannot do this thing, to give our sister to one who is uncircumcised, for that would be a disgrace to us. [15] Only on this condition will we consent to you: that you will become as we are and every male among you be circumcised. [16] Then we will give our daughters to you, and we will take your daughters for ourselves, and we will live among you and become one people. [17] But if you will not listen to us and be circumcised, then we will take our daughter and be gone. "

Praise and Worship: "Lord I Lift Your Name on High."
Second Scripture Reading: Genesis 34:18-24
Glenn Johnson

[18] Their words pleased Hamor and Hamor's son Shechem. [19] And the young man did not delay to do the thing, because he was delighted with Jacob's daughter. Now he was the most honored of all his family. [20] So Hamor and his son Shechem came to the gate of their city and spoke to the men of their city, saying, [21] "These people are friendly with us; let them live in the land and trade in it, for the land is large enough for them; let us take their daughters in marriage, and let us give them our daughters. [22] Only on this condition will they agree to live among us, to become one people: that every male among us be circumcised as they are circumcised. [23] Will not their livestock, their property, and all their animals be ours? Only let us agree with them, and they will live among us." [24] And all who went out of the city gate heeded Hamor and his son Shechem; and every male was circumcised, all who went out of the gate of his city.

Welcome and Statement of Purpose: Rev. Marcia Grayson –
(Thank You and dinner and post-surveys.)
Third Scripture Reading:Genesis 34:25-31Collete Jackson

> [25] On the third day, when they were still in pain, two of the sons of Jacob, Simeon and Levi, Dinah's brothers, took their swords and came against the city unawares, and killed all the males. [26] They killed Hamor and his son Shechem with the sword, and took Dinah out of Shechem's house, and went away. [27] And the other sons of Jacob came upon the slain, and plundered the city, because their sister had been defiled. [28] They took their flocks and their herds, their donkeys, and whatever was in the city and in the field. [29] All their wealth, all their little ones and their wives, all that was in the houses, they captured and made their prey. [30] Then Jacob said to Simeon and Levi, "You have brought trouble on me by making me odious to the inhabitants of the land, the Canaanites and the Perizzites; my numbers are few, and if they gather themselves against me and attack me, I shall be destroyed, both I and my household. " [31] But they said, "Should our sister be treated like a whore?"

Selection: Selection: "Open Heaven"
Sermon: "What's Love Got to Do With It?" Genesis 34
Altar call and Prayer
Offering: Deacons
Benediction

Public Information

Rev. Marcia Grayson, Doctoral Candidate at New Brunswick Theological Seminary, presents her research project sermon series.
"Using Transformational Preaching to Bring Awareness and Break the Silence in Congregations Regarding Sexual and Physical Abuse Against Women."

Join us each Wednesday evening for our Worship services
February 6th, 20th, 27th, and March 6, 2019
From 6:00 PM - 7:00 PM
Second Baptist Church
124 Atkins Avenue, Asbury Park, NJ.
Dr. Semaj Y. Vanzant, Sr., Pastor-Teacher...

Bibliography

Aldrich, Joe. *Lifestyle Evangelism: Learning How to Open Your Life to Those Around You.* New York: Multnomah, 1981.

Allen, Holly Catterton and Christine Lawton Ross. *Intergenerational Christian Formation: Bringing the Whole Church Together in Ministry, Community and Worship.* Downers Grove: InterVarsity Press, 2012.

Anderson, Herbert, and Edward Foley. *Mighty Stories, Dangerous Rituals: Weaving Together the Human and the Divine.* San Franciso: Jossey-Bass, 2001.

Anthony, Micheael J., ed. *Christian Education: Foundations for the Twenty-first Century.* Grand Rapids: Baker Academic, 2001.

Assualt, South Eastern Center Against Sexual. *South Eastern CASA.* March 13, 2017. https://www.secasa. com.au/pages/feelings-af-ter-sexual-assault/ (accessed 06 06, 2018).

Bailey, Randall C. , Tat-siong Benney Liew, and Fernando F. Segovia, eds. *They Were All Together in One Place?: Toward Minority Biblical Criticism.* Atlanta: Society of Biblical Literature, 2009.

Baucham, Voddie Jr. *Expository Apologetics: Answering Objections with the Power of the Word.* Wheaton: Crossway, 2015.

Birch, Bruce C. , Walter Brueggemann, Terence E. Fretheim, and David L. Peterson. *A Theological Introduction to The Old Testament.* Nashville: Abingdon Press, 2005.

Blount, Brian K., gen.ed. , Cain Hope Felder, Clarice J. Martin, and Emerson B. Powery, assoc. eds. *True to Our Native Land:*

An African American New Testament Commentary. Minnapolis: Fortress Press, 2007.

Booth, Wayne C., Gregory G. Colomb, Joseph M. Williams, Joseph Bizup and William T. Fitzgerald. *The Craft of Research.* Chicago and London: The University of Chicago Press, 2016.

Branson, Brenda and Paula J. Silva. *Violence Among Us: Ministry to Families.* Valley Forge: Judson Press, 2007.

Brown, Sally A. and Luke A. Powery. *Ways of the Word: Learning to Preach for Your Time and Place.* Minneapolis: Fortress Press, 2016.

Bryant-Davis, Thema, ed. *Surviving Sexual Violence: A Guide to Recovery and Empowerment.* Lanham: Rowman and Littlefield, 2011.

Byasse, Jason. "How Churches are Reaching Out: Gangs and God. " *Christian Century*, September 18, 2007: 20-27.

Cairns, James. *The Myth of the Age of Entitlement: Millennials, Austerity, and Hope.* Toronto: University of Toronto Press, 2017.

Chapell, Bryan. *Christ-Centered Preaching: Reedeming te Expository Sermon.* Grand Rapids: Baker Academic, 2005.

Cohen, Cathy J., Matthew Fowler, Vladimir E. Medenica and Jon C. Rogowski, eds. "The "Woke" Generation? Millennial Attitudes on Race in the US." *GenFoward Surveys*, 2017: 1-45.

Coleman, Monica A. *Making a Way Out of No Way: A Womanist Theology.* Minneapolis : Fortress Press, 2008.

Cooper-White, Pamela. *The Cry of Tamar: Violence against Women and the Church's Response. Second Edition.* Minneapolis: Fortress Press, 2012.

Cosgrove, Charles H. and W. Dow Edgerton. *In Other Words: Incarnational Translation for Preaching.* Grand Rapids: William B. Eerdmans , 2007.

Crumpton, Stephanie M. *A Womanist Pastoral Theology Against Intimate and Cultural Violence.* New York: St. Martin's Press LLC, 2014.

Curtis, Miranda. "Open Heaven." *Open Heaven: The Miranda Experience Live.* Columbia / Fair Trade Services, 2018.

Davis, H. Grady. *Design for Preaching.* Minneapolis : Fortress Press, 1958.

Deacon Nourse, Bill, Ed. D. "billnourse. com." *http://www.bill-nourse. com/4SOURCE. HTM.* April 22, 2003. http://www.bill-nourse. com (accessed October 6, 2017).

Dyson, Michael Eric. *Tears We Cannot Stop: A Sermon to White America.* New York: St. Martin's Press, 2017.

Edwards, Jr. O.C. *A History of Preaching.* Nashville: Abingdon Press, 2004.

Ellingsen, Mark. *Integrity of Biblical Narrative: Story in Theology and Proclamation.* Eugene: Wipf and Stock, 1990.

Eugene, Toinette M., and James Newton Poling. *Balm For Gilead: Pastoral Care for African American Families Experiencing Abuse.* Nashville: Abingdon Press, 1998.

Felder, Cain Hope. *The Original African American Heritage Study Bible.* Valley Forge: Judson Press, 1993.

Flake, Elaine M. *God in Her Midst: Preaching Healing to Wounded Women.* Valley Forge: Judson Press, 2007.

Francis, Pope. *The JOY of the GOSPEL.* New York: Image, 2013.

Furtick, Steven. *(Un)Qaulified How God Uses Broken People To Do Big Things.* Colorado Springs: Multnomah Books, 2013.

Gambino, Childish. *This is America.* Cond. Donald and Ludwig Goransson Glover. Comp. Donald Glover. 2018.

Gould, Meredith. *The Social Media Gospel: Sharing the Good News in New Ways, Second Edition.* Collegeville: Liturgical Press, 2015.

Guder, Darrell L., ed. *Missional Church: A Vision for the Sending of the Church in North America.* Grand Rapids: William B. Eerdmans Publishing Company, 1998.

Heyboer, Kelly and Ted Sherman. "NJ.com True Jersey." *nj.com.* February 13, 2019. http://www.nj.com (accessed February 26, 2019).

Hopkins, Anna. "Fox News." *foxnews.com.* January 13, 2019. http://www.foxnews.com (accessed February 26, 2019).

Horowitz, Jason and Elizabeth Dias. "The New York Times." *nytimes.com.* February 5, 2019. http://www.nytimes.com (accessed February 26, 2019).

Hurd, Stephen. *The Seed of David: A Worshipper's Guide to Mend the Heart and Discipline the Flesh.* Newark: Godzchild, 2015.

Idleman, Kyle. *Not a Fan. Becoming A Completely Committed Follower of Jesus.* Grand Rapids: Zondervan, 2011.

Jackson, Kevin. "American Thinker." *https://www.americanthinker.com* . June 15, 2010. https://www.americanthinker.com/articles/2010/06/the_slave_mentality.html#ixzz5ipm8LnAF (accessed March 21, 2019).

Jerry, Carter. Dr. ""Shaping Narrative Preaching."" n.d.

Joyner, Randy L., Wiliam A. Rouse, and Allan A. Glatthorn. *Writing the Winning Thesis or Dissertation: A Step-By-Step Guide.* Thousand Oaks: Corwin, 2013.

Keller, Timothy. *Preaching: Communicating Faith in an Age of Skepticism.* New York: Viking, 2015.

King, Daphne L. "The Lived Experience wit Christianity and Teenage African- American Female's Perceptions of Their Self-Esteem." *Christian Education Journal 3. 12. 1*, 2015: 45-57.

KJV. *Life Application Study Bilbe*. Wheaton, IL: Tyndale House Publishers, 1989.

Krebs, Christpher Ph.D. , Christine Lindquist, Marcus Berzofsky, Bonnie E. Shook-Sa, M.A. S., Kimberly Peterson, RTI International, Michael G. Planty, Ph.D. , Lynn Langton, Ph.D. , Jessica Stroop, Bureau of Justice Statistics. *Bureau of Justice Statistics*. January 20, 2016. Christopher Krebs, Ph.D. , Christine Lindquist, Marcus Berzofsky, Bonnie E. Shook-Sa, M.A. S., Kimberly Peterson, RTI International, Michael G. Planty, Ph.D. , Lynn Langton, Ph.D. , Jessica Stroop, Bureau of Justice Statistics (accessed August 21, 2018).

Leslie, Kristen J. "When Violence is No Stranger: Pastoral Care and Acquaintance Rape. " *Journal of Religion and Abuse 3*, 2001: 77-78.

Lim, Stephen, D. Min. "Preaching That Actually Changes Lives: 6 Keys in Forming Disciples." *Enrichment Journal*, 2013.

Lisher, Richard. *Theories of Preaching: Selected Readings in the Homiletical Tradition*. Durham: The Labyrinth Press, 1987.

Lowery, Eugene. *How to Preach a Parable: Designs for Narrative Sermons*. Nashville: Abingdon Press, 1989.

Lozado, Francisco, Jr. and Greg Carey, eds. *Soundings in Cultural Criticism: Perspectives and Methods in Culture, Power, and Identity in the New Testament*. Minneapollis: Fortress Press, 2013.

Luckerson, Victor. "Millennials cant afford to be color-blind about race. " *The View*, July 20, 2015: 25-26.

Mananzan, Mary John, Mercy Amba Oduyouye, Elsa Tamez, J. Shannon Clarkson, Mary C. Grey, and Letty M. Russell, eds. *Women Resisting Violence: Spirituality for Life.* Maryknoll: Orbis Books, 1996.

Mann, Mary Ellen. *From Pain to Power: Overcoming Sexual Trauma and Reclaiming Your True Identity.* Colorado Springs: WaterBrook Press, 2015.

McCary, P.K. *Black Bible Chronicles Series: Rappin with Jesus, The Good News According to the Four Brothers.* NY: African American Family Press, 1994.

McClure, John S., Ronald J. Allen, Dale P. Andrews, L. Susan Bond, Dan P. Moseley, and G. Lee Ramsey, Jr. *Listening to Listeners: Homiletical CASE STUDIES* . St. Louis: Chalice Press, 2004.

McDill, Wayne. *http://www.lifeway.com/pastors/2014/03/12/7-principles-of-biblical-interpretation/.* March 03, 2014. http://www.lifeway.com (accessed September 30, 2017).

McDowell, Sean. *Apologetics for a New Generation: A Biblical and Cuturally Relevant Approach to Talking.* Eugene: Harvest House, 2009.

McKenzie, Vashti M. *Journey to the Well.* Chicago: Urban Ministries, Inc. , 2002.

McKinney, Lora-Ellen. *View From the Pew: What Preachers Can Learn from Church Members.* Valley Forge: Judson Press, 2004.

McLean, B. H. *Biblical Interpretation and Philisophical Hermeneutics.* New York: Cambridge University Press, 2012.

McMickle, Marvin A. *Where Have All the Prophets Gone? Reclaiming Prophetic Preaching in America.* Cleveland: The Pilgrim Press, 2006.

Miles, Reverend Al. *Domestic Violence: What Every Pastor Needs to Know.* Minneapolis: Fortress Press, 2000.

Mumford, Debra J. Ph.D, and Frank H. Caldwell. "Slave Prosperity Gospel." *Special Issue: Black Homiletics and Economics 41, no.1,* 2016: 31-41.

Neuger, Christie Cozad. *Counseling Women: A Narrative, Pastoral Approach.* Minneapolis: Augsburg Fortress, 2001.

Nieman, James R., and Thomas G. Rogers. *Preaching to Every Pew: Cross Cultural Strategies.* Minneapolis: Fortress Press, 2001.

Nouwen, Henri J. M. *The Wounded Healer: Ministry in Contemporary Society.* New York: Image Doubleday, 1972.

Organization, World Health. *World Health Organization.* November 29, 2017. https://www.who.int/en/news-room/fact-sheets/detail/violence-against-women (accessed December 18, 2018).

Ortberg, John. "Biblical Preaching is About Life Change, Not Sermon Style. " *Preaching Today,* 2010.

Patterson, Carol Lynn. "Evangelism: Fulfilling Our Commitment to Witness." *Calvery Connection,* n.d. : 5.

Peterson, Eugene H. *The Message Study Bible.* Colorado Springs: NavPress, 2012.

Phillips, Kristine and Amy B. Wang. "The Washington Post." February 10, 2019. https://www.washingtonpost.com/religion/2019/02/10/pure-evil-southern-baptist-leaders-condemn-decades-sexual-abuse-revealed-investigation/ (accessed February 17, 2019).

Poling, James Newton Ph.D and Christie Cozad Neuger, Ph.D, eds. *Men's Work in Preventing Violence Against Women.* Binghamton: Haworth Pastoral Press, 2002.

Proctor, Samuel D. *The Certain Sound of the Trumpet: Crafting a Sermon of Authority.* Valley Forge: Judson Press, 1994.

Quicke, Michael. "History of Preaching: Assessing Today's Preaching in Light of History." *The Arts and Craft of Biblical Preaching*, 2005: 64-69.

Rainer, Thom S. and Jess W. Rainer. *The Millennials: Connecting to America's Largest Generation*. Nashville: B & H, 2011.

Rainer, Thom S. *I Am A Church Member*. Nashville: BH Publishing Group, 2013.

Robinson, Haddon and Craig Brian Larson, eds. *The Art and Craft of Biblical Preaching: A Comprehensive Resource for Today's Communicators*. Grand Rapids: Zondervan, 2005.

Robinson, Haddon W. *Biblical Preaching: The Development and Delivery of Expository Messages, Third Edition*. Grand Rapids: Baker Academic, 2014.

Sanday, Peggy Reeves. *Fraternity Gang Rape: Sex, Brotherhood, and Privilege on Campus*. New York: New York University Press, 2007.

Savage, Carl and William Presnell. *Narrative Research in Ministy: A Postmoen Resarch Approach for Faith Communities*. Louisville: Wayne E. Oates Institute, 2008.

Science, Religion, and Culture Harvard Divinity School. *Interrogating the Silence: Religious Leaders' Attitudes towards Sexual and Gender-based Violence*. Final, Harvard Divinity School, Cambridge: Harvard Divinity School, 2015.

Sensing, Tim. *Qualitative Research: A Multi-Method Approach to Projects for Doctor of Ministry*. Eugene: Wipf & Stock, 2011.

Sheres, Ita. *Dinah's Rebellion: A Biblical Parable For Our Time*. New York: Crossword, 1990.

Sinozich, Sofi, Lynn Langton, Ph.D. , Bureau of Justice Statistics. *Bureau of Justice Statistics*. December 11, 2014. http://www.

bjs.gov/index.cfm?ty=pbdetail&iid=5176 (accessed August 21, 2018).

Smith, Fred. "A Prophetic Christian Education for Black Boys: Overcoming Violence. " *Black Theology: An Interactive Journal.* 1. 2, 2003: 175-187.

Smith, Mitzi J., ed. *I Found God in Me: A Womanist Biblical Hermenuetics Reader.* Eugene: Cascade Books, 2015.

Sojourners, IMA World Health and. *IMA World Health.* June 2014. https://imaworldhealth.org/wp-content/uploads/2014/07/PastorsSurveyReport_final1. pdf (accessed December 17, 2018).

St. Clair, Raquel. "Womanist Biblical Interpretation." *True to Our Native Land: An African American New Testament Commentary,* 2007: 54-62.

Stanley, Andy. "The Art and Craft of Biblical Preaching." *Bridging the Marketplace Gap,* 2005: 680-681.

Stevenson-Moessner, Jeanne and Teresa Snorton. *Women Out of Order: Risking Change and Creating Care in a Multicultural World.* Minneapolis: Fortress Press, 2010.

Stone, Robin D. *No Secrets, No Lies: How Black Families Can Heal From Sexual Abuse.* NY: Broadway Books, 2004.

Sweetham, John. "NCLS Research." *NCLS.org.* n.d. http://www.ncls.org.au/default.aspx?sitemapid=1057 (accessed March 23, 2017).

Ter Kuile, Casper. "Millennials Haven't Forgotten Spirituality, They're Just Looking For New Venues." *PBS New Hour.* March 3, 2017.

The Center for Family Justice: Statistics . n.d. https://centerforfamilyjustice. org (accessed January 17, 2019).

The Center for Generational Kinetics. *The Center for Generational Kinetics.* 2016. genhq.com (accessed April 8, 2018).

Thompson, Lisa L. *Ingenuity: Preaching as an Outsider.* Nashville: Abingdon Press, 2018.

Tracy, Natasha. *Healthy Place for Your Mental Health.* May 26, 2016. https://www.healthyplace. com/abuse/rape/types-of-rape-the-different-forms-of-rape (accessed April 08, 2019).

Voelz, Richard W. *Youthful Preaching: Strengthening teh Relationship Between Youth, Adults, and Preaching.* Eugene: Cascade Books, 2016.

Vyhmeister, Nancy Jean and Terry Dwain Robertson. *Your Guide to Writing Quality Research Papers: For Students of Religion and Theology.* Grand Rapids: Zondervan, 2014.

Wallace, H. *http://www.hwallce. unitingchurch.org.au.* n.d. http://www.hwallce. unitingchurch.org.au (accessed October 6, 2017).

Webber, Robert E. *Ancient-Future Evangelism: Making Your Church a Faith-Forming Community.* Grand Rapids: BakerBooks, 2003.

Webber, Robert E. *Journey to Jesus: The Worship, Evangelism, and Nurture mission of the Church.* Nashville: Abbingdon Press, 2001.

West, Carolyn M. and Kalima Johnson. "National Online Resource Center on Violence Against Women." *VAWnet.org.* March 2013. https://vawnet.org/sites/default/files/materials/files/2016-09/AR_SVAAWomenRevised. pdf (accessed November 23, 2018).

West, Steven D. *Resurrection, Scripture, and Reformed Apologetics: A Test for Consistency in Theology and Apologetic Method.* Eugene: Pickwick Publications, 2012.

West, Traci C. *Wounds of the Spirit: Black Women, Violence, and Resistance Ethics.* New York and London: New York University Press, 1999.

Wiese, Bill. *23 Minutes In Hell: One Man's Story About What He Saw, Heard, and Felt in that Place of Torment.* Lake Mary: Charisma House, 2006.

Willimon, William H. and Richard Lisher, eds. *Concise Encyclopedia of Preaching.* Louisville: Westminister John Knox Press, 1995.

Wilson, Paul Scott. *Preaching and Homiletical Theory.* St. Louis: Chalice Press, 2004.

Women of Color Network. *Women of Color Network.* June 2006. www.doj.state. or.us/wp-content/uploads/2017/08/women_of_color_network_facts_domestic_violence_2006. pdf (accessed January 17, 2019).

CPSIA information can be obtained
at www.ICGtesting.com
Printed in the USA
LVHW010736021121
702214LV00009B/342